OECD
ECONOMIC
SURVEYS

2000-2001

Spain

OECD

ORGANISATION FOR ECONOMIC CO-OPERATION AND DEVELOPMENT

ORGANISATION FOR ECONOMIC CO-OPERATION AND DEVELOPMENT

Pursuant to Article I of the Convention signed in Paris on 14th December 1960, and which came into force on 30th September 1961, the Organisation for Economic Co-operation and Development (OECD) shall promote policies designed:

- to achieve the highest sustainable economic growth and employment and a rising standard of living in Member countries, while maintaining financial stability, and thus to contribute to the development of the world economy;

- to contribute to sound economic expansion in Member as well as non-member countries in the process of economic development; and

- to contribute to the expansion of world trade on a multilateral, non-discriminatory basis in accordance with international obligations.

The original Member countries of the OECD are Austria, Belgium, Canada, Denmark, France, Germany, Greece, Iceland, Ireland, Italy, Luxembourg, the Netherlands, Norway, Portugal, Spain, Sweden, Switzerland, Turkey, the United Kingdom and the United States. The following countries became Members subsequently through accession at the dates indicated hereafter: Japan (28th April 1964), Finland (28th January 1969), Australia (7th June 1971), New Zealand (29th May 1973), Mexico (18th May 1994), the Czech Republic (21st December 1995), Hungary (7th May 1996), Poland (22nd November 1996), Korea (12th December 1996) and the Slovak Republic (14th December 2000). The Commission of the European Communities takes part in the work of the OECD (Article 13 of the OECD Convention).

Publié également en français.

Table of contents

Assessment and recommendations   9

I. Macroeconomic performance   23

  Macroeconomic developments: the economy is cooling off   23
  A supportive macroeconomic policy led to strains in the economy   42
  Challenges for fiscal policy in the medium term   50
  The fiscal stability law   53
  Prospects   54

II. Reform options to boost sustainable growth   57

  Labour market reforms   64
  Product market reforms   71
  Financial market reforms   85
  Public sector issues   92

III. Ensuring the long-term financial viability of the pension system   99

  The ageing process will occur later but will be more severe than in other countries   100
  Institutional arrangements for supporting the elderly   106
  The impact of ageing on public finances   129
  The options for reform   133

Notes   142

Glossary of acronyms   155

Bibliography   156

Annexes

  I. Changes to the method of calculating the consumer price index   161
  II. The liberalisation package of June 2000   162
  III. Recent labour market reform measures   165
  IV. Uncertainties regarding the demographic projections   166
  V. The Toledo Pact: measures to improve the public pension system and their impact   168
  VI. Internal rate of return of the public pension system   169
  VII. Corporate supplementary pension systems: pension funds and insurance contracts   172
  VIII. Calendar of main economic events   174

List of boxes

  1. Recent and future changes in the labour force survey methodology   35
  2. What is the potential growth of the Spanish economy?   38
  3. Has the "new economy" arrived in Spain?   58
  4. The fertility decline   101
  5. The recent reform of the public pension system   107
  6. The pension scheme for central government civil service employees   113
  7. Maintaining prosperity in an ageing society: recommendations for Spain   140

List of Tables

  1. Financial position of the economic sectors   26
  2. Financial performance of non-financial firms   27
  3. Balance of payments   31
  4. Labour productivity growth   36
  5. Potential output growth   37
  6. Inflation decomposition: comparison between Spain and the euro area   40
  7. The fiscal consolidation process   45
  8. General government accounts   49
  9. Stability Programme 2000-04   51
 10. Short-term prospects   55
 11. Recommendations for further structural reform   60
 12. EPL: severance payments   67
 13. International comparison of bank profitability   86
 14. Public employment and transfer recipients   93
 15. Health care system indicators   96
 16. Evolution of pharmaceutical expenditure   97
 17. Public pension schemes: number of pensions and expenditure   106
 18. Main parameters of public pension schemes in selected countries   110
 19. Retirement age and contribution duration for earnings-related pension schemes   114
 20. Replacement rates and rates of return for the main earnings-related
     pension schemes   115
 21. Replacement rates and rates of return for the general pension scheme   117
 22. Expenditure of earnings-related pension schemes   117
 23. Implicit tax rates for an extra year of work   121
 24. Comparison of pensioners' income in selected OECD countries   124
 25. Comparison of old-age care and health systems   127
 26. Components of pension expenditure until 2050   132
 27. Implications of changing certain parameters of the general pension scheme   133

Annex

A1. Demographic projections   166

List of Figures

  1. Recent consumption indicators   24
  2. Household demand and saving ratio   25
  3. Unit labour costs and prices by sector   28
  4. Contributions to GDP growth   30
  5. Competitiveness indicators and export performance   32
  6. Employment and unemployment: key features   34
  7. Consumer prices   41
  8. General government budget   43

9.	The macroeconomic policy stance	44
10.	The government deficit and the structural budget balance	46
11.	Total factor productivity growth	57
12.	Temporary employment contracts by sector	64
13.	Part-time employment in international perspective	65
14.	Incidence of unemployment by age and sex	65
15.	State aid in EU countries	74
16.	Telephone charges in selected countries	77
17.	Internet subscribers in the OECD area	78
18.	Electricity prices in selected OECD countries	81
19.	Bank intermediation margins and profitability	87
20.	Private venture capital investment	92
21.	Comparison of health care expenditure in OECD countries	95
22.	Fertility rates and life expectancy	102
23.	Population trends in Spain and old-age dependency ratios	103
24.	Labour market situation	104
25.	Immigration: an international comparison	105
26.	Pension expenditure in selected countries	111
27.	Pensions benefiting from the minimum complement	112
28.	Participation rates for population aged 55-64	119
29.	Pension expenditure projections	130

BASIC STATISTICS OF SPAIN (2000)

THE LAND

Area (1 000 km²):		Major cities (1998, thousands inhabitants):	
Total	506.0	Madrid	2 882
Cultivated (1996)	191.4	Barcelona	1 506
		Valencia	739
		Sevilla	702

THE PEOPLE

In thousands:		Employment (thousands)	14 474
Population	39 442	Employment by sector (% of total):	
Net natural increase	27	Agriculture	6.8
Net migration	40	Industry	19.9
Number of inhabitants per km²	77.9	Construction	11.0
		Services	62.3

PRODUCTION

Gross domestic product (GDP):		Gross fixed capital investment:	
Billion ESP	100 873	% of GDP	25.4
Per head (US$)	14 187	Per head (US$)	3 602

THE GOVERNMENT

% of GDP:		Composition of Parliament (number of seats):	350
Consumption	17.1	Popular Party (PP)	182
Revenue	38.4	Spanish Workers' Socialist Party (PSOE)	125
Deficit	−0.3	Convergence and Union (CIU)	15
Fixed investment (% of gross fixed capital		United Left (IU)	8
formation)	12.9	Basque Nationalist Party (PNV)	7
		Other	13
		Last general elections: March 2000	

FOREIGN TRADE

Exports of goods and services (% of GDP)	29.9	Imports of goods and services (% of GDP)	32.2
Exports as a % of total goods exports:		Imports as a % of total goods imports:	
Foodstuffs	11.4	Foodstuffs	6.0
Other consumer goods	28.5	Other consumer goods	18.8
Energy	3.1	Energy	12.0
Other intermediate goods	43.6	Other intermediate goods	45.3
Capital goods	13.3	Capital goods	18.0

THE CURRENCY

Monetary unit: Peseta		Currency units per US$, averge of daily figures:	
Fixed conversion rate to euro:		Year 2000	180.5
1 euro = ESP 166.386		April 2001	186.2

Note: An international comparison of certain basic statistics is given in an annex table.

Assessment and recommendations

Activity remained buoyant in 2000, but tensions have emerged

Overall, 2000 was another favourable year for the Spanish economy. Activity remained buoyant for the fourth successive year and the growth differential with the euro area was again positive, though it narrowed somewhat. Especially heartening was the continuation of brisk job creation, employment expanding more rapidly than in most other OECD countries. Despite this favourable overall picture, tensions have started to build up which could compromise the sustainability of the current expansion: the financial position of the private sector has weakened over the last years; inflationary pressures have mounted with the closing of the output gap; and productivity gains have remained very weak.

Domestic demand has slowed considerably, but has been offset by higher net exports so far

After several years of strong expansion, domestic demand slowed markedly during the course of last year, decelerating from a rate of more than 5 per cent at end-1999 to under 3 per cent in the second half of 2000. The financial position of households has weakened considerably in recent years, so that when real income was dented last year by the rise in oil prices and consumer confidence shaken by the fall in stock market values, private consumption growth slowed. Corporate indebtedness has also increased over the past few years and the rise in energy and labour costs and the turnaround in interest rates have dented operating surpluses, even though profitability remains strong. Businesses have cut back sharply their investment in machinery and equipment and have taken a wait-and-see attitude in the face of mounting uncertainties about future economic developments. Despite the slowdown in domestic demand, output growth remained close to 4 per cent as the improved external environment significantly boosted net exports.

Unemployment has fallen again, but productivity gains have remained meagre

Although job creation lost some momentum, the growth of employment remained impressive, bringing the unemployment rate down further to 13.4 per cent in early 2001. But the decline in the number of job seekers has slowed, partly because of a rise in labour force participation. Structural reforms to product and labour markets have clearly been important in generating strong employment growth. But the impact of structural reform on productivity is not yet visible at the aggregate level. Indeed, productivity growth slowed in recent years and remained very weak in 2000. As a result, there is no clear evidence yet that the economy's potential output growth has increased. The buoyant activity in recent years has thus led to a progressive tightening of markets, with the output gap turning positive in 2000. Nevertheless, taking into account the structural reforms implemented by the Spanish authorities, and in line with other countries' recent experience, Spain should benefit from both a pick up in productivity and output potential in coming years.

Inflation accelerated, reflecting the oil price rise, the effect of the "mad cow" disease and the emergence of bottlenecks

Inflation accelerated to 4 per cent at end-2000, partly owing to the energy price rise and the euro's depreciation. Consumer price inflation remained close to 4 per cent in April 2001 despite the recent dip in oil prices. Rising inflation has been driven by special factors, but has also reflected high capacity utilisation and rising labour costs. Underlying inflation has drifted up since the middle of last year and is now among the highest in the euro area. Wage growth also picked up in 2000, because of the activation of the pay indexation clauses that are included in an increasing number of wage agreements, and, in some sectors and regions, because of tightening labour market conditions. This has resulted in higher unit labour costs and output prices in the sheltered sectors, while profit margins decreased in the sectors that are exposed to foreign competition. These developments suggest that the widening inflation differential with the euro area is not simply a matter of real convergence. Persistence of such a differential could erode the economy's competitiveness over time, though at present Spanish competitiveness remains good and Spain has continued to gain market shares, although in a less impressive way than in previous years. Though the current account deficit widened to over 3 per cent of GDP (Gross

Domestic Product) in 2000, this is mainly due to terms-of-trade losses and not weakening competitiveness.

A supportive macroeconomic policy stance led to strains in the economy

The pace of domestic demand has slowed even though the macroeconomic policy stance has remained supportive. Monetary conditions in Spain, which eased markedly in the period leading up to and following the adoption of the euro, have stayed relaxed despite the successive interest rate hikes by the European Central Bank since end-1999. With higher inflation than in most other euro area countries, real interest rates are still low and credit growth has remained very rapid. While, as measured by the structural deficit, fiscal policy did tighten since 1997, this has not significantly offset the easing of monetary conditions. Over this period, the actual budget deficit declined substantially and indeed by more than foreseen by the authorities, as cyclical developments accentuated the structural improvement. In 2000 the general government deficit fell by a further 0.9 per cent of GDP to 0.3 per cent with higher-than-expected revenues only partly used to meet increased spending obligations. The 2001 Budget, which was designed assuming a growth rate of 3.6 per cent, aims to bring the general government account into balance for the first time in 25 years. Despite the fact that the official growth projection has been revised down to 3.2 per cent, the objective to achieve a balanced budget has been maintained.

The slower pace of activity in 2001 will probably not be sufficient to lower underlying inflation, and fiscal policy should be vigilant

In the OECD's projections, output growth slows significantly to around 3 per cent in 2001 and 2002, which would be close to the economy's growth potential. The deceleration reflects a slowdown in both domestic and foreign demand. Households and businesses, whose consumption and investment have already weakened significantly since mid-2000, will probably continue to exercise caution because of the mounting economic uncertainties and the deterioration in their financial position. Even though the OECD's growth projections are less optimistic than those of the government, the balanced budget target should be achievable since the official revenue projections are very cautious. The improvement in the general government account will have a marginal damping effect on demand, and by itself will probably not be sufficient to slow underlying inflation significantly. Consistent also with long-term requirements, some additional tightening of the fiscal stance may be necessary. On the other hand, uncertainties as to the scale of the slowdown in activity are large. This will depend both on developments in the external environment, which may become even less favourable, and on the behaviour of households and businesses, whose confidence may decline further. Such downside risks weaken the immediate case for fiscal tightening and rather suggest that fiscal settings will need to be assessed carefully in the light of economic developments.

Pursuit of a sound fiscal policy in the medium term will necessitate additional efforts to control expenditure

Spain's Stability Programme aims at keeping the general government account in slight surplus (¼ per cent of GDP) between 2002 and 2004 and at reducing the general government debt by 7 percentage points of GDP. In addition to maintaining a small surplus, which should allow sufficient room for manoeuvre to counter adverse shocks, the programme provides for a further cut in the personal income tax as of 2003. The programme foresees continued brisk growth of capital expenditure to boost infrastructure development, while further restraint on current expenditure is planned in order to reduce total public expenditure as a percentage of GDP. Finally, it is planned to use the social security surpluses to increase the resources of the social security reserve fund (to 1 per cent of GDP). Overall, the medium-term strategy adopted by the authorities is not ambitious enough, especially as it rests on an economic growth assumption of 3.2 per cent a year until 2004, which is probably a little optimistic. However, it is worth noting that even with more moderate growth the authorities are committed to keep a balanced budget. The intended reduction in the share of current expenditure will necessitate additional efforts to control spending programmes, such as pensions and pharmaceuticals, which have been growing rapidly in recent years.

The draft legislation on fiscal stability is timely but carries certain risks

A fiscal stability bill has been put forward to establish a framework for fiscal discipline in a country, which is among the most decentralised in the OECD. Such a rule may be appropriate as a measure to accelerate the development of a culture of "fiscal responsibility" at all levels of government and will help to meet the requirement of long-term fiscal sustainability. It would prohibit deficit financing of public expenditure at all levels of government as from 2003 in order to lock in the favourable fiscal performance of the last years. Deficits would not be ruled out altogether but would be confined to temporary and exceptional situations. They would have to be duly justified and budget-balancing plans would have to be put before Parliament. Compliance by each budgeting entity would be monitored through a statistical information system permitting greater transparency, and penalties might be imposed. The proposed legislation is a means to reinforce fiscal discipline at a time when strong public finances might otherwise tend to encourage higher expenditure and lower taxation. The improved information requirements and increased transparency are also a step forward. Yet this legislation carries certain risks, if applied too rigidly. This fiscal rule would seem to necessitate the maintenance of substantial budget surpluses by all levels of governments to leave them scope to deal with cyclical developments, and as such is much more constraining than the rule laid down in the Stability and Growth Pact for Spain as a whole. Insofar as such surpluses were not achieved there would be a risk that automatic stabilisers could not fully function in the event of a steep downturn. However, the meaning of an "exceptional situation" has yet to be clarified and could provide an escape clause for difficult situations, albeit at the expense of reducing the credibility of the rule.

Reforms are essential to prepare Spain for the consequences of population ageing

A strict fiscal rule should add pressure to reform the pension system, which is discussed in the special chapter of this *Survey*. Reforms are indeed essential to prepare Spain for the difficulties that will stem from the ageing of its population. Although occurring relatively late, as from 2020-25, the demographic shock will be particularly severe and its expected impact on pensions has not been lessened by the 1997 and March 2001 reforms of the social security's pay-as-you-go system. There will also be ageing-related pressures on health care expenditure and social services. The fact that the current financial balances of the various pension schemes are satisfactory overall, and will probably continue to be so for several years, should not mislead policymakers. The present parameters of the old-age pension system are more generous than in most other OECD countries and public expenditure on pensions could increase by some 8 percentage points of GDP between now and 2050. A whole range of measures will be needed to ensure the sustainability of the public finances in the face of these prospects. The extent of future reform requirements will, however, depend on overall fiscal discipline in the future. In this context, the new social security reserve fund and the fiscal stability bill are useful first steps. The strategy of reducing debt or building up assets before the demographic shock occurs should be part of the response to the problems linked with ageing. But the effectiveness of such a strategy tends to be limited by the uncertainties inherent in the budgeting process, which is set in a much more narrow time frame and is inevitably influenced by political considerations.

The pension system should be made less generous

To keep the retirement pension schemes in balance, the rate of return on workers' contributions has to be lower than the long-term rate of economic growth, which is not the case at present. Raising contribution rates today to prefund rapidly rising expenditure in the future would be a risky solution as it would be very difficult to resist political pressure to spend such revenues on further increasing the generosity of the public pension system. In addition, this approach by raising labour costs would have negative effects on employment. In view, in particular, of labour market consequences, it would seem preferable to focus on measures to reduce the effective cost of the pay-as-you-go system, rather than increasing the funding. The parameters of the retirement pension calculation therefore need to be revised. Various adjustments should be envisaged. These could include basing pensions on earnings over a whole career instead of the last 15 years, raising the number of contribution years for a full pension from 35 to 40, and lowering the earnings replacement rate from its current level of close to 100 per cent for a full contribution career. This reduction of generosity should apply to all schemes and their rules should be harmonised. Reduced generosity should not translate into poverty for the elderly because its negative impact on pension levels should be offset by the positive effect resulting from the likely improved employment history of future pensioners. This would be ensured by the gradual phasing in of the reduction in generosity.

Disincentives to stay in the labour force should be eliminated

Another set of measures should aim at keeping elderly workers in the labour market. Financial incentives to retire before the statutory age of 65 pose problems that need to be addressed. The incentives offered to State employees are very generous and should be cut back. In the case of the general regime, the recent decision to extend the possibility to retire early for those over 61 and unemployed for over six months makes it all the more important to move quickly to an actuarially neutral system for low-income workers as well as those with a long contribution period. In this regard, the recent cut in the pension-reduction coefficient in the case of early retirement does not help for this latter group. On the other hand, the decision to exempt employers from contributing to the social security system for workers over 65 will raise their employability, but this should be accompanied by greater incentives for workers to stay in the labour force. In this respect, the new possibilities for cumulating part of wages and pensions after age 65 are welcome.

Making the private pension system compulsory might be considered

The private pension system could also be developed further. It is a fully-funded system, capable of serving as a useful complement to the public pay-as-you-go system, and its broadening would boost capital markets if aggregate savings were to rise as a result. The development of private pension plans could also add a new dimension to bargaining and would probably ease wage pressure if awards also covered pension rights. The authorities might consider making this second pillar of the pension system compulsory. A stronger funded pension pillar would partly offset the reduced generosity of the public pension regime and bring greater flexibility to the overall system. Further efforts should be devoted to improving the regulatory framework for the operation of pension funds, in particular to strengthen competition.

Increasing the rate of employment will help in the long term only if the pension system's generosity is reduced

Measures to increase labour force participation could also help to solve the economic difficulties associated with population ageing. But if these measures are to be effective in the long term, the pension system's generosity must be reduced. Otherwise they will merely postpone the problem of pension financing. Measures to augment the labour supply could include increased immigration and reforms to reduce unemployment and to raise the labour market participation of women. The development of services catering for the demand of couples for child care centres and social services to help them reconcile family and working life would be useful to bring more women into the labour force. The development of more flexible part-time work contracts will also help to increase female employment further while improved job prospects for the young could raise the birth rate, which has been very low in recent years, hence rebalancing the demographic structure.

Social services are inadequate and need to be developed

The ageing process will increase the demand for social assistance to the dependent elderly, which at present is chiefly provided informally by families. These informal arrangements are being progressively undermined by the decline in the number of children able to take care of their parents, the growing complexity of care for the aged and the trend increase in female participation in the labour market. It is therefore necessary to increase the as yet insufficient supply of social services with flanking policies to reduce interregional disparities and to encourage the development of non-institutionalised assistance. Home care, for example, is currently in very short supply. At the same time it is important to prevent the mounting demand for these services from causing a steep rise in budget costs, as could happen if supply is skewed towards forcing the elderly into rest homes or even hospitals. Another question to be resolved is access to social services at affordable prices, given the limited financial resources of the elderly. Solutions like service vouchers, flexibly combining public and private financing, and the development of a private insurance system are complementary approaches that could be pursued.

Decentralisation has regained momentum

Control of health care spending, which will also be subjected to upward pressure because of the ageing process, is another major fiscal issue. Already seven Autonomous Communities manage health care and the others may follow soon. The authorities have recently focused their efforts on pharmaceutical expenditures, which have risen very steeply. The reforms, including cuts in pharmacists' mark-ups and the introduction of a reference pricing system, have brought encouraging results, but other measures will be necessary if there is to be a lasting shift in the trend. A firm control of health expenditure is important for the financial health of the Autonomous Communities. These regional administrations are responsible for an increasing share of public expenditure, which as of 2001 also includes education spending. The reform of their financing, which is now under discussion and should take effect in 2002, is therefore of particular importance. This reform aims to provide stable resources for regions while improving fiscal co-responsibility in the context of the fiscal stability bill. It is important that this will not lead to higher overall taxation. The options to transfer additional taxation powers from the State to the Communities are limited. For instance, the transfer of indirect taxation would conflict with the need to preserve the internal market, which is subject to EU rules. However, increased recourse to user charges should be envisaged, particularly with respect to local authorities.

A further relaxation of employment protection legislation is necessary

Reflecting high unemployment, the labour market has for years been one of the main targets of structural reform. By reducing severance costs and employers' social contributions for hiring the most marginalised workers on permanent contracts, the 1997 labour market reform contributed to the impressive employment growth of recent years. Despite this progress, the share of temporary employment has remained very high, suggesting that at the margin even the new "special" permanent contracts are viewed as too constraining by employers. At the same time, there is some evidence that temporary employment is detrimental to skill formation and may therefore account partly for the meagre productivity performance. With the 1997 provisions about to expire, the authorities renewed them in March 2001 and extended them to other categories of workers, so that now only men between the ages of 30 and 45 are still ineligible for the special permanent contracts. In addition, temporary workers are now entitled to severance pay, which might lead to an increase in permanent contracts but could have negative effects on job creation in some sectors. Overall, these measures have only a limited impact on employment protection, which is still more constraining than in most other OECD countries. Hence, a general reduction of severance pay for permanent contracts that applies to all workers, down to levels in countries with high employment rates, remains desirable. Severance allowances could also be lowered in aggregate if the distinction between a "fair" and "unfair" dismissal was based on criteria that prevented the courts from finding the majority of dismissals to be unfair. While the reform of job protection has advanced little, the measures adopted in March 2001 have eased the regulation of part-time contracts, which were formerly very rigid. The proportion of part-time contracts should therefore increase, bringing more women into the labour market and perhaps encouraging less frequent recourse to temporary work contracts.

The collective bargaining system should be simplified

Other reforms will be needed to raise employment and lower structural unemployment, which is still among the highest in the OECD. The collective bargaining system warrants priority here. The present system operates at multiple levels, thus introducing an inflationary bias *via* successive add-ons, while the industry-wide agreements take insufficient account of productivity performance at the enterprise level. A shift towards more decentralised bargaining to allow firms greater flexibility would be desirable. Furthermore, an increasing number of agreements include inflation catch-up clauses that should be phased out. Other reforms should focus on improving the public employment service, which intermediates in only a small proportion of new work contracts and whose recent devolution to the Autonomous Communities has generated difficulties of co-ordination. More effort should also be devoted to the assessment of active labour market policy programmes; the evidence from various OECD countries is that if such programmes are well-designed, and carefully targeted, they should improve the employability of marginal workers to some extent. An independent assessment of the effectiveness of the present programmes would be useful. Finally, it is important to reduce the industrial accident rate, which is high in international comparisons.

Regulatory reform has progressed, but concentration is still inhibiting market forces

The OECD's 2000 *Review of Regulatory Reform in Spain* has pointed out many ways that would lead to a better regulatory framework and greater competitive pressures. Regulatory reform is a major element of the economic strategy of the government and has indeed continued to progress rapidly resulting in lower energy and telecommunications prices. In June 2000, a comprehensive set of new regulatory measures were taken to improve the organisation of certain markets, which included raising transparency and reducing vertical integration in the energy sector. In the electricity and hydrocarbon sectors, restrictions were placed on the expansion of dominant groups during the next few years and complete deregulation of the electricity sector was brought forward to 2003. In the gas sector, where the established monopoly is now exposed to competition in certain segments of the market, full liberalisation will now also take place by 2003. Measures were also taken to stimulate competition in hydrocarbon distribution. Despite these measures the energy sector is still marked by concentration and the lack of interconnection with European networks, an obstacle the government would like to see removed. This is particularly the case with electricity, where prices, despite a sharp fall, are still high. A break-up of the two leading companies in this sector, together with separation of generation from distribution activities should be envisaged. Regulatory reform has progressed significantly in the telecommunications sector, notably with the opening of the local loop. This should encourage connections to the Internet, which is as yet little used in Spain even though the number of regular users doubled over the past 12 months, spurred by the measures adopted. In this sector, marked by technological change and a rapid evolution of market organisation, the authorities should try to develop a framework conducive to investment.

The resources and powers of the regulatory authorities should be increased

In recent years the government has created an environment more favourable to competition. An ambitious programme of privatisation has been carried out and on a number of occasions the government has limited concentrations. A phasing-out of the last remaining public monopolies, like the railways as of 2002, is now scheduled. To consolidate these favourable developments, more powers and resources should be transferred to the regulatory bodies responsible for assessing competition and enforcing appropriate behaviour where market failures are present. The competition authorities, which have played an active and important role in recent years, have insufficient resources. The telecommunications market commission should also have its competencies extended, notably in the mobile telephony sector. Moreover, the potential for distortions of competition generated by subsidies to industry could be further reduced if this aid were redirected to horizontal objectives like support for research and develop-ment. In agriculture, the subsidies delivered by the government – *via* transfers to the pension scheme, reduced value added tax on fuel oil, and a water price that is often very low – appear excessive. If water were priced closer to its cost, this would limit subsidies to the agricultural sector and would give a better signal of future infrastructure requirements, which have recently been drawn up in the national water plan.

Prudential
supervision of
banks must
remain vigilant

Banking consolidation progressed throughout the 1990s, especially in the case of commercial banks, whose balance sheet structure has come closer to that of banks in other countries with lower operating costs and smaller intermediation margins. The merger process in com-mercial banking that began in the early 1990s may have reached completion with the emergence of two pre-eminent institutions, but banks have continued to expand through acquisitions abroad, especially in Latin America. In the sav-ings bank sector, the consolidation process of the many small regionally-controlled establishments should continue. Bank supervision has remained vigilant and further steps have been taken to improve credit risk evaluation. The authorities should continue to pay particular attention to the risks associated with the development of bank invest-ments in Latin America, given the uncertainties concerning economic developments in that region. Capital market and investment fund regulation should continue to aim at increased harmonisation with the other European countries so as to derive greater benefits from the integration process under way. Finally, it is necessary to determine whether the effects of the recent reform of venture capital regulations are sufficient for Spain to catch up in this area, venture capi-tal being one of the keys to higher productivity.

Summing-up

Spain's favourable growth performance has been accompanied by the emergence of inflationary pressures. Easy monetary conditions since Spain entered the monetary union have raised demand above productive capacity in 2000 despite a tightening of fiscal policy, and underlying inflation has drifted up. Wage and price moderation are essential if competitiveness is to be maintained and if activ-ity and employment are to expand sustainably, especially since productivity gains continue to be small. Given these underlying inflationary tensions, the slowdown of activity that seems likely to occur in 2001 appears necessary. The improvement in the general government account will have a marginal damping effect on demand, and by itself will probably not be sufficient to slow underlying inflation significantly. Consistent also with long-term requirements, some additional tightening of the fiscal stance may be necessary. However, downside risks to activity weaken the immediate case for a fiscal tightening. At this stage of the cycle, it is important not to overestimate the economy's potential growth. The positive effects of the reforms undertaken are clearly evident in terms of employment creation, but they have not boosted productivity thus far. Recent reforms in the product, capital and labour markets and in the budgeting process have been moves in the right direction, but in some cases the advances have been limited. Efforts to increase competition should be maintained and labour market rigidities reduced, in particular by a reform of wage bargaining mechanisms and a further softening of employment protection legislation. New reforms are also needed to prepare Spain for the consequences of population ageing, an area where perceptions among the social partners have not yet fully caught up with the rather stark long-term unsustainability of current arrangements. Overall, the most recent reform is not likely to improve the financial viability of the public pension system. A whole range of complementary measures will have to be introduced to ensure adequate incomes for the elderly, while respecting the financing constraints imposed by long-term productive capacity. Furthermore an increase in the supply of social services to the elderly will be necessary. A rapid and determined start to reforms that would include reducing the pension system's generosity and eliminating the disincentives to prolonging working life is necessary to establish the sustainability of public finances in the long term. It is important to take advantage of the still favourable economic situation to get these reforms underway as well as to advance the structural reform agenda. Ensuring macroeconomic stability and pursuing structural reforms are necessary to increase growth potential and accelerate the convergence with high income countries.

I.   Macroeconomic performance

Economic growth remained buoyant in 2000, reaching about 4 per cent for the fourth successive year. Spain thus maintained a positive growth differential with the euro area average, although the gap has narrowed.[1] The pace of domestic demand slowed significantly, however, but this was largely offset by an increase in net exports underpinned by stronger foreign demand. The unemployment rate continued to fall and in early 2001 stood at 13.4 per cent, as against 15.0 per cent a year earlier, and employment continued to grow relatively briskly. Although wage growth was fairly moderate, labour costs rose more rapidly, because productivity gains were small. This, together with the oil price rise and the emergence of some strain on capacity, caused inflation to accelerate throughout 2000. Despite somewhat lower oil prices at the beginning of 2001, consumer price inflation remained at 4 per cent in April. But underlying inflation, which is at 3.4 per cent, has drifted upward since the middle of last year, and the differential with the euro area average has widened.

Monetary conditions are still easy for the Spanish economy's cyclical position, despite the interest rate rises by the European Central Bank (ECB) since late 1999 and the slight pick-up in the euro at end-2000. With inflation rising more rapidly than in most other countries of the euro area, real interest rates are still low. The structural deficit has declined since 1997 but this has not significantly offset the easing of monetary conditions. Demand has been expanding more rapidly than the economy's growth potential and production is now slightly above capacity. Despite the still relaxed stance of macroeconomic policy, output growth is expected to slow significantly to about 3 per cent in 2001 and 2002, which will probably be insufficient to slow underlying inflation. Uncertainties concerning the scale of the slowdown are however large. Hence, the key question is whether the economy will slow sufficiently to reduce the strains in the economy and curb inflationary pressures. It is therefore important to keep economic developments under close scrutiny. Consistent also with long-term requirements, some further tightening of fiscal policy may be necessary. However, downside risks to activity weaken the immediate case for a fiscal tightening.

Macroeconomic developments: the economy is cooling off

Household spending has weakened

Private consumption grew by 4 per cent on average in 2000. As in previous years, robust growth was buoyed by the rise in household disposable income as employment levels continued to climb. The household saving ratio was also lower than in 1999, household confidence being boosted by falling unemployment. Yet the average for 2000 conceals a marked change in the course of the year. Between the first and last quarters of 2000 consumption growth slowed, from an annual rate of 5 per cent to 2¾ per cent. A number of factors were responsible for the sharp deceleration. First of all, the impact of the personal income tax cuts introduced by the 1998 tax reform wore off. Second, the ECB interest rate rises curbed car purchases, more than two-thirds of which are financed by credit, during the second half of the year (Figure 1).[2] Third, the increased cost of mortgage credit reduced liquidity for purchases of other durables, which had risen steeply in previous

Figure 1. **Recent consumption indicators**

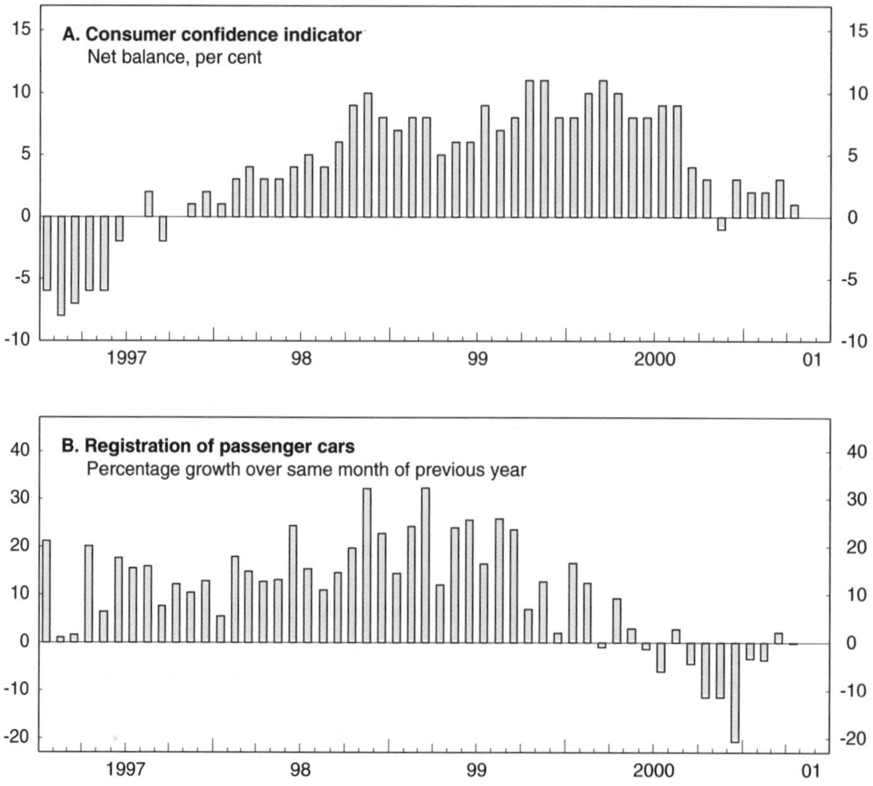

Source: Ministry of Economy, Eurostat and ANFAC.

Figure 2. **Household demand and saving ratio**

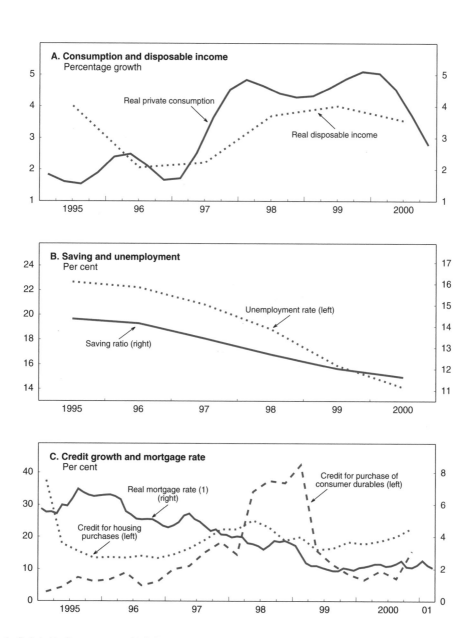

1. Deflated by the consumer price index.
Source: Bank of Spain; Ministry of Economy and OECD, *Main Economic Indicators.*

years (Figure 2). Finally, as from autumn, the oil price rise and the stock market decline reduced income and wealth, as well as confidence which had reached a historically high level in mid-2000.[3] Over the past five years net lending of households has decreased considerably (Table 1). On the one hand, the saving ratio, which has declined steadily as the economic situation improved, is now at a historically low level. On the other hand, home purchases have continued at a brisk pace. The latter probably reflects pent-up demand by young persons, a large number of whom have found employment at a time when real interest rates on home loans are still low. Indeed, low interest rates since Spain joined monetary union in 1999 helped to sustain strong growth of mortgage credit (Figure 2).

Table 1.   **Financial position of the economic sectors**

Per cent of GDP

	1996	1997	1998	1999	2000[1]
Gross saving					
Total economy	22.1	22.6	22.6	22.3	22.4
Financial corporations	1.6	1.3	1.5	1.0	1.3
General government	−1.2	0.4	1.2	2.8	3.4
Non-financial firms	11.9	11.7	11.4	10.5	10.2
Households[2]	9.9	9.2	8.5	8.0	7.6
Capital transfers and investment					
Total economy	−20.8	−21.0	−22.1	−23.5	−24.7
Financial corporations	−0.6	−0.6	−0.4	−0.5	−0.6
General government	−3.7	−3.6	−3.8	−3.9	−3.8
Non-financial firms	−11.5	−11.8	−12.6	−13.4	−14.1
Households[2]	−5.1	−5.0	−5.3	−5.6	−6.2
Net lending					
Total economy	1.2	1.6	0.5	−1.1	−2.2
Financial corporations	1.0	0.7	1.1	0.5	0.7
General government	−4.9	−3.2	−2.6	−1.2	−0.3
Non-financial firms	0.4	−0.2	−1.3	−2.9	−3.9
Households[2]	4.8	4.2	3.2	2.4	1.4

	2000			
	Q1	Q2	Q3	Q4
Net financial transactions				
Total economy	−2.8	−2.2	−2.3	−1.5
Financial corporations	1.3	1.0	1.2	−0.8
General government	1.0	2.4	−0.4	−4.2
Non-financial firms	−2.6	−3.6	−6.6	0.4
Households[2]	−2.5	−1.9	3.4	3.1

1. Estimates.
2. Including non-profit institutions serving households.
Source: INE, Bank of Spain and IGAE (Intervención General de la Administración del Estado).

Business investment growth has slowed significantly

The brisk growth of business investment, which averaged 9¼ per cent in 1998 and 1999, slowed to under 6 per cent in 2000. The deceleration continued throughout the year and was more marked for machinery and equipment than for construction, with investment growth in the former category declining from over 8½ per cent at the beginning of 2000 to 1½ per cent in the last quarter. This sharp slowdown occurred despite capacity utilisation and profits remaining high.[4] Corporate profitability improved during the last few years, largely as a result of moderate wage claims and declining financial costs.[5] Since mid-1999, however, corporate profit margins have narrowed somewhat even if they remain high by historical standards. The rise in labour costs and energy prices has not been completely offset by higher output prices. Furthermore, although real interest rates are still at low levels, the fact that they have been rising again has ended the favourable influence that financial cost reduction exerted since the mid-1990s. Profitability developments have differed across sectors. Margins decreased principally in industry, also reflecting increased competition from other euro area producers (Figure 3). In construction, on the other hand, higher production costs were more than offset by substantial price increases, which points to the emergence of a marked dichotomy between the sheltered and exposed sectors of the economy. Overall, businesses have increased their indebtedness to finance their investment in recent years (Table 2). Given the downward trend in share prices due to the turbulence on stock markets, debt-equity ratios have also risen. Since

Table 2. **Financial performance of non-financial firms**[1]

Per cent

	Annual sample			Quarterly sample				
				1999	2000			
	1997	1998	1999	Q4	Q1	Q2	Q3	Q4
Growth, annual rate								
Gross value added	7.1	6.8	4.3	2.7	7.2	8.2	8.3	11.8
Labour costs	4.0	5.7	5.3	4.9	6.3	5.8	5.3	2.2
Financial costs	−13.6	−7.0	−3.0	0.5	12.9	13.3	40.2	48.8
Net result[2]	14.8	16.6	17.0	9.7	28.2	25.9	33.3	−6.4
Profitability ratios								
Net income[2]	7.7	8.9	8.2	7.6	8.3	9.2	10.7	10.3
Debt ratio[2]	39.0	39.9	43.6	44.3	42.0	41.5	42.1	44.9
Leverage ratio[3]	0.8	3.1	3.1	2.3	3.0	3.7	4.5	3.8

1. Data coverage is biased towards large, public and industrial enterprises.
2. As a per cent of gross value added.
3. Rate of return of assets less financial costs on total liabilities (in percentage points).
Source: Bank of Spain, Central de Balances.

Figure 3.   **Unit labour costs and prices by sector**
Percentage change over same quarter of previous year[1]

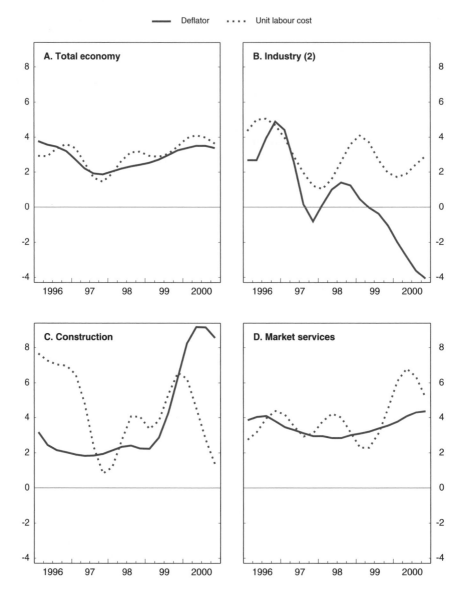

1. National accounts, trend-cycle adjusted data.
2. Mining and manufacturing.
Source: INE, Ministry of Economy and OECD.

enterprises do not appear to face financing problems so far, recent investment behaviour no doubt reflects caution prompted by uncertainty about future developments in the economy.

Stronger net exports have offset the slowing of domestic demand

The deceleration of private consumption and investment spending was matched by still moderate general government consumption due to the maintenance of the restrictions limiting recruitment. Consequently, growth of total domestic demand slowed appreciably, from an annual rate of over 5 per cent in 1998 and 1999 to 3 per cent in the fourth quarter of 2000. While imports weakened accordingly, there was a marked pick-up in net exports thanks to a more favourable external environment, notably in the countries of the European Union, and somewhat increased international competitiveness as the euro lost ground. The contribution of net exports to activity, which was still negative at the beginning of 2000, increased progressively, and this offset the weakening of domestic demand and allowed output growth to keep running at 4 per cent throughout the year (Figure 4).

The current balance has deteriorated because of the oil bill

Since the second half of 1999, Spain's external performance was shaped by the marked acceleration of international trade, the steep oil price rise and the weakening of the euro, which lost an average of 13½ per cent against the dollar in 2000 (although Spain's nominal effective exchange rate fell only by 3 per cent). The cyclical gap between Spain's economy and that of its main trading partners, which had caused a deterioration of the current account position between 1997 and 1999, narrowed in 2000, but this did not lead to an improvement in the external balance. The current deficit actually widened again to reach 3.1 per cent of GDP in 2000 against 2.1 per cent in 1999, chiefly owing to the oil price rise and the euro's depreciation, which caused a loss of 3 percentage points in the terms of trade (Table 3). The rise in the oil bill, which amounted to nearly 1½ per cent of GDP, accounted for more than 80 per cent of the increase in the trade deficit between 1999 and 2000 (on a customs basis). With demand less buoyant, imports grew slightly less rapidly than in 1999 but still increased by over 10 per cent on average in 2000. The higher surplus of the tourism account limited the deterioration in the current balance. Nevertheless, there was some slowdown in the growth of net tourism receipts by comparison with previous years, owing to increased competition from other countries. Tourism prices rose comparatively rapidly in 2000, which somewhat eroded the competitiveness of this sector.

Export price competitiveness improved only slightly in 2000 (around 1 per cent), despite the euro's sharp depreciation (Figure 5, Panel A). The gain in competitiveness is very small compared with that of German and French producers

Figure 4.   **Contributions to GDP growth**[1]

Percentage change over same quarter of previous year

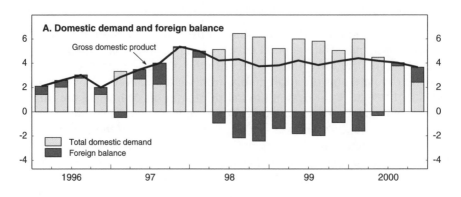

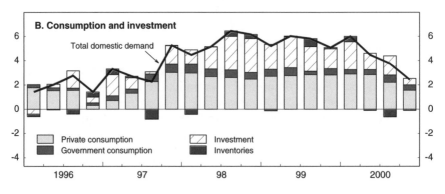

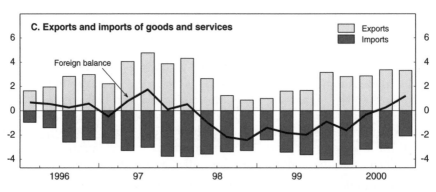

1. Seasonally adjusted data.
Source: OECD, *Quarterly National Accounts* and INE.

Table 3. **Balance of payments**

In million euros

	1997	1998	1999	2000
Trade balance	−11 802	−18 480	−28 585	−35 643
(as a % of GDP)	−2.4	−3.5	−5.1	−5.9
Non-factor services (excluding tourism)	−2 112	−2 689	−3 726	−3 526
Tourism	19 695	22 315	25 250	27 743
Net investment income	−5 949	−6 751	−8 904	−9 055
Net current transfers	2 408	3 006	2 853	1 523
Current balance	2 240	−2 598	−13 112	−18 959
(as a % of GDP)	0.5	−0.5	−2.3	−3.1
Capital balance	5 609	5 680	6 552	5 217
Financial balance (net change)[1]	−2 783	−105	11 242	21 509
Assets (net change)	37 299	67 162	84 368	136 698
Spanish investment abroad				
Direct	11 041	17 002	39 501	58 303
Portfolio and financial derivatives	14 407	41 521	43 816	62 960
Other investment[2] and reserve assets	11 850	8 639	1 051	15 435
Liabilities (net change)	34 516	67 057	95 609	158 207
Foreign investment in Spain				
Direct[3]	5 621	10 592	14 791	39 742
Portfolio[4]	11 067	15 400	42 688	62 212
Other investment[2]	17 828	41 065	38 130	56 253
Errors and omissions (net)	−5 066	−2 977	−4 682	−7 768
Memorandum items				
Terms of trade, goods and services (% change)	−0.1	0.9	−0.1	−3.0
As a % of GDP				
Foreign direct investment in Spain	1.1	2.0	2.6	6.6
Direct investment abroad	2.2	3.2	7.0	9.6
Net direct investment	1.1	1.2	4.4	3.1

1. Changes in financial assets and liabilities are both net of repayments. Financial derivatives have been included in the change in financial assets although they are obtained as the balance of assets less liabilities.
2. Mainly loans, deposits and repo operations.
3. Does not include direct investment in listed shares but includes portfolio investment in non-listed shares.
4. Includes direct investment in listed shares but does not include portfolio investment in non-listed shares.
Source: Bank of Spain and OECD.

(5 to 7 per cent). The marked improvement (9 percentage points) in Spain's relative export prices against countries outside the euro area was nearly offset by a slight deterioration (under 1 point) against euro area competitors.[6] In terms of price level, however, Spanish exports remain fairly competitive relative to the European average, even though they have lost some ground in recent years. In fact, Spain has only marginally increased its export market share during the last years (Figure 5, Panel B). This less favourable development may also reflect a shift in the internationalisation process of the economy. Whereas formerly the driving

Figure 5. **Competitiveness indicators and export performance**

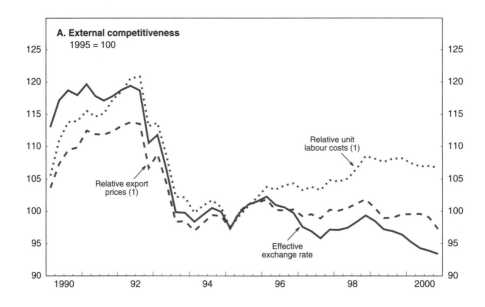

A. External competitiveness
1995 = 100

Relative unit labour costs (1)

Relative export prices (1)

Effective exchange rate

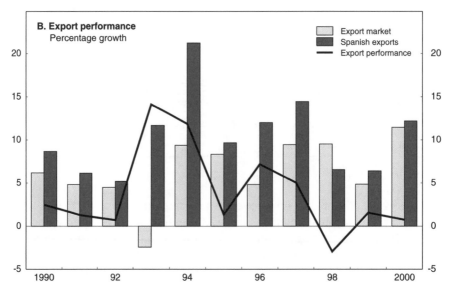

B. Export performance
Percentage growth

☐ Export market
■ Spanish exports
— Export performance

1. Manufacturing.
Source: OECD.

force was a rapid expansion of foreign trade, since 1997 there has been a significant rise in outward direct investment, which has now overtaken inward direct
investment. In 1999 and 2000, outward direct investment, mainly to Latin America,
represented on average more than 8¼ per cent of GDP a year, compared with
2¾ per cent in 1997-98 (Table 3). If the increase in inward investment is factored
in, the net capital outflow amounted to more than 3¾ per cent of GDP on average
in the last two years, against around 1 per cent in 1997 and 1998.

Employment growth is still buoyant, although a little slower

Growth of employment was again remarkable in 2000, extending the positive results recorded since 1997. It averaged 4.2 per cent after correction of the
statistical changes introduced last year (Figure 6 and Box 1). Although the rate of
job creation lost some momentum during the year,[7] 491 000 jobs were created
between the last quarter of 1999 and the last quarter of 2000. In early 2001,
employment increased by 2.8 per cent in the first quarter (on a year-on-year
basis). As before, job creation in the construction sector was especially strong.
More of the new jobs went to women than to men and more to persons over 55
and to youth than to other age groups. The factors underpinning employment creation were the favourable business climate, the continuation of wage restraint and
the still perceptible impact of the 1997 labour market reform. However, the effects
of this reform, which *inter alia* provides for standardised permanent contract
recruitment of young and elderly persons and the long-term unemployed, showed
signs of wearing off. The number of new subsidised contracts decreased in 2000,
after the steep increase recorded between 1997 and 1999, owing in part to a
reduction in the extent to which social security contributions are reduced for such
workers (see Chapter II for more details).[8] Although the number of permanent jobs
rose more rapidly than that of temporary jobs, the latter's share of total employment decreased only slightly: it amounted to 31.5 per cent in early 2001, which is
only 2 percentage points less than in 1997 and twice the European average.[9] The
share of part-time employment, amounting to 8.2 per cent, has not increased
since 1997 and remains lower than the OECD average.

Labour force growth amounted to 2.0 per cent in 2000, twice the rate
recorded in the years from 1997 to 1999. The increase is mainly attributable to the
pick-up in participation rates for women aged 25 to 54 and persons aged over 55,
whose employment prospects have improved. This rise in participation slowed
the decline in unemployment: the jobless rate, which stood at 13.6 per cent in the
fourth quarter of 2000, declined by 1.8 percentage points in the course of the year,
as against 2.8 percentage points the previous year. The unemployment rate continued to fall in early 2001, reaching 13.4 per cent in the first quarter. The slowdown of job creation at the beginning of the year was offset by the weakening of
labour force growth, which amounted to 1.0 per cent (on a year-on-year basis) in

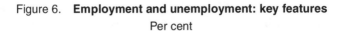

Figure 6.   **Employment and unemployment: key features**

Per cent

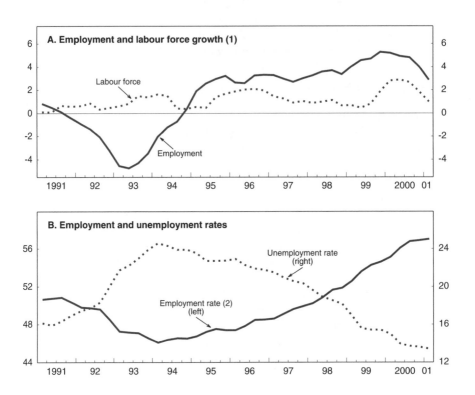

1. Seasonally adjusted; growth over same quarter of previous year.
2. Employment as a per cent of population aged 16-64.
Source: INE, Ministry of Economy and OECD.

the first quarter of 2001. The rate of decline in unemployment weakened steadily throughout 2000 and in early 2001[10] and the unemployment rate is still appreciably higher than the OECD average. But part of the gap, which amounted to 8 percentage points in 2000, reflects a difference of definition that should be corrected by the next revision of the labour force survey scheduled for the beginning of 2002 (Box 1). As in previous years, the reduction in the number of the jobless chiefly benefited the more marginal workers with little or eroded job experience and often limited training. In 2000, the reduction in unemployment was twice as steep for first-time job seekers and the long-term unemployed as for other

Box 1. Recent and future changes
in the labour force survey methodology

Several changes have been made to the employment and unemployment statistics in the labour force survey since 1995. The aim of these changes was to update the sample with a view to making it more representative and to bring the methods of recording unemployment more into line with those of Eurostat. These changes continued in 2000 and further amendments, outlined below, are due to be introduced in early 2002.

During the first quarter of 2000, part of the survey sample (4 per cent) was updated to make it more representative of the distribution of the population across the country. As in the last update in 1995-96, this change made it possible to obtain a more accurate picture of the trend of employment in urbanised areas. Its effect was to increase recorded employment by 77 500 persons (mainly employees on indefinite contracts), and the participation rate by 0.26 percentage point. The number of unemployed and the unemployment rate were affected only marginally.

Three major changes will affect employment statistics in 2002:

– First, the way the number of unemployed is counted will be changed to make it consistent with Eurostat rules. Thus, to be counted as unemployed, people will have to show that they have been actively looking for a job. More specifically, two conditions will have to be met: *i*) they must have been in contact with the unemployment office (INEM) within the previous four weeks (at present, they only have to be in contact with it every three months); *ii*) they must have taken steps to find a job (contact with the unemployment office for administrative reasons will not be considered valid except when the person first signs on as a job-seeker).

– Second, new population projections are going to be used to take account of the recent increase in the immigrant population, so that the reference population used will be larger.

– A new adjustment (reweighting) will be applied to allow for the fact that the replies for the 25-40 year-old age groups in the sample population under-represent the actual numbers.

The impact of these three changes on employment and unemployment statistics is difficult to evaluate. A parallel survey to be carried out in 2001 will make it possible to quantify their impact early in 2002.

The most significant of the three changes is the new definition of unemployment. According to the National Statistical Institute, the number of people affected potentially by this change, who at present are counted as being unemployed solely because they are registered with the INEM, would be 700 000 at the most. Only some of them would not meet the new definition of unemployment. If half of this population is excluded from the statistics, the unemployment rate should fall by 2¼ percentage points. Employment will not be affected and the number of inactive persons will increase. The use of new population projections should increase the number of jobs, unemployed and inactive persons, but should not affect the participation and unemployment rates. Lastly, it is expected that the reweighting will increase employment and the participation rate of the population.

workers. The share of long-term unemployment in total unemployment fell from 55.6 per cent at the end of 1997 to 47.8 per cent in the first quarter of 2001. During that period the decline in the number of job seekers, which averaged 31 per cent, was nearly 40 per cent among persons with primary education or less and around 27 per cent for those with secondary or higher education. On the other hand, 61 per cent of the people leaving unemployment during the period belonged to the category with secondary or higher education.[11]

Productivity growth has remained weak. Although productivity gains may be somewhat underestimated owing to problems of measurement,[12] it is clear that these have slowed significantly since the mid-1990s as the employment situation has improved.[13] This trend, which is also evident in other European countries, has been particularly marked in Spain despite a continuing potential for productivity catch-up with the main trading partners (Table 4). The entry of the least productive workers into the production process and into traditionally low-productivity sectors would appear to be largely responsible for this phenomenon.[14] Although the labour market reform has permitted strong job creation, this has been obtained at the cost of decelerating productivity. In fact there are doubts on whether the economy's output potential has increased in recent years, despite the reforms that have reduced structural unemployment and raised the employment rate (Table 5 and Box 2). It is likely that this period of low productivity growth is temporary, given the recent

Table 4.   **Labour productivity growth**

Output per person employed

	Average growth over period			Change (points) (b – a)
	1987-2000	1987-94 (a)	1994-2000 (b)	
Spain	1.6	2.3	0.8	−1.5
Belgium	1.8	1.9	1.7	−0.2
Finland	2.7	2.8	2.7	−0.1
France	1.6	1.8	1.3	−0.5
Germany[1]	1.6	2.0	1.2	−0.8
Ireland	3.6	3.4	3.8	0.5
Italy	1.7	2.0	1.4	−0.6
Netherlands	1.3	1.7	0.9	−0.8
United Kingdom	1.5	1.6	1.5	−0.1
Euro area[1]	1.6	1.9	1.2	−0.7
United States	1.5	1.1	1.9	0.8
Japan	1.7	1.9	1.4	−0.5
OECD	1.7	1.7	1.7	0.1

1. West Germany up to 1991 inclusive.
Source: OECD.

Table 5. **Potential output growth**

Percentage change

	1985-2000	1985-94	1994-2000	Output gap level in 2000
OECD estimate	2.9	2.9	2.8	0.3
of which, contribution of:				
Capital stock	1.0	1.1	1.0	..
Trend labour efficiency	1.1	1.2	0.9	..
Potential employment	0.8	0.7	1.0	..
of which:				
Working-age population	0.5	0.6	0.3	..
Trend participation rate	0.4	0.3	0.5	..
Structural unemployment	−0.1	−0.3	0.2	..
Memorandum items				
IMF estimate	2.9	2.9	3.0	0.5
EC estimate	2.9	2.8	3.2	0.8

	1986	1995	2000
OECD NAIRU[1] estimate	15.0	16.5	14.2

1. Non-accelerating inflation rate of unemployment.
Source: OECD; IMF (2000), *World Economic Outlook* and European Commission.

structural reform efforts. On the other hand, there is nothing that indicates that it has come to an end. This implies that it will be crucial to preserve wage moderation so as not to penalise the economy's competitiveness.

Inflation has accelerated with the oil price rise and the emergence of bottlenecks

Higher labour costs have pushed up output prices. This is indicated in Table 6, which shows a breakdown of inflation (measured by the GDP deflator) since 1995 into labour cost, indirect taxation and corporate profits for Spain and the euro area.[15] Nominal wages per employee rose more sharply in 2000, partly because of the progressive tightening of the labour market. Although the unemployment rate remains high on average, it was in fact relatively low in some regions (about 6 per cent in Navarra and Baleares, and 7 per cent in Aragon and La Rioja). In agriculture, tourism and construction, labour shortages have emerged, but this was largely met by increased recourse to immigration. On the other hand, in activities related to the new technologies it has become more difficult to satisfy labour demand. Furthermore, surveys indicate that unemployed persons are less prepared than before to accept a change of residence or a lower-skilled job in order to become employed. The fact that pay agreements contain indexation clauses is another reason for the steeper rise in wages in 2000. An increasing number of collective agreements

Box 2.   **What is the potential growth of the Spanish economy?**

Growth has averaged over 4 per cent since 1997. Given the major changes that have taken place in the economy since the mid-1990s, it is important to evaluate to what extent this expansion reflects a cyclical catch-up after the deep recession of 1992-93 or a trend increase in potential output growth. Spanish growth in recent years, which has been accompanied by the creation of a large number of jobs and low productivity growth, depends on strict wage restraint being maintained. It is thus important to ensure that excessive demand pressures are not put on productive capacity, which would jeopardise growth. In particular, it is necessary to adopt a macroeconomic policy stance that is appropriate with regard to Spain's cyclical position.

Unfortunately, growth of potential cannot be observed and all such estimates need to be interpreted with caution. Several estimation methods exist, all with advantages and disadvantages: purely statistical techniques of smoothing time series, or more economic approaches which use production functions whose determinants (potential employment, capital and total factor productivity) are estimated with various semi-structural or statistical methods. The OECD uses the second type of approach, which makes it possible to better identify the various determinants of potential supply and the level of production compatible with non-inflationary growth.

Estimates of potential growth over the recent period differ depending on the approach used and are subject to a large degree of uncertainty. Estimates obtained by purely statistical methods, like the Hodrick-Prescott (HP) filter used by the European Commission, could give different results than approaches that use a production function (OECD) depending on the cyclical path.[1] However, care has to be taken with estimates derived from purely statistical techniques, like the HP filter, since they tend to be affected by a significant end-of-period bias, which, in the case of Spain, is positive because of the strong growth in recent years. Hence, these methods have to be interpreted with great caution as regards the most recent developments. On the other hand, production functions also tend to be backward looking because of the way parameters are estimated. These methods have difficulties to capture recent structural changes.

The results of these estimates are presented in Table 5. They show that the potential growth of the economy has been nearly 3 per cent of GDP since 1986, the year Spain joined the European Union. However, there appears to have been no acceleration since 1995 compared with the period 1985-94.[2] Given the strong growth in recent years all estimates (OECD, IMF, European Commission) agree that there was a positive output gap in 2000, although the estimates differ as to its size.

The OECD's estimate of potential output growth takes into account the various factors that have influenced supply conditions in the economy in recent years. The first of these factors is the reform of the labour market, which has reduced structural unemployment or the NAIRU, from 16½ per cent in 1995 to 14¼ in 2000 (OECD, 2000), and increased the trend participation rate. Both have helped to

---

Box 2.   **What is the potential growth of the Spanish economy?** (*cont.*)

increase the potential supply of labour during the period 1995-2000. This positive trend was however partly offset by slower growth of the working-age population due to the population ageing process, even allowing for the recent increase in immigration. Despite the rise in investment since 1995, the contribution of the increase in the capital stock to potential growth is estimated to have varied only slightly over the 1985-2000 period.[3] In contrast, the slowdown of labour efficiency has restrained the increase in potential.

According to the OECD's estimate, potential output growth could remain at slightly under 3 per cent in the next few years. This estimate, which is based on the assumption of a continuous fall of structural unemployment to about 12 per cent in 2005, incorporates a slightly stronger growth of trend labour efficiency. It is lower than the growth assumption of 3¼ per cent adopted by the authorities in their new Stability Programme for 2000-04.

---

1. The Commission uses two measures of the output gap. Besides the HP filter which is mainly used for the purpose of calculating cyclically-adjusted balances, it also calculates a measure of potential output based on a production function as used in the macro-econometric model QUEST II and derives from that a measure of the output gap. The estimates of the output gap for Spain in the year 2000 are 0.9 per cent according to the HP filter and 1.2 per cent according to the production function approach (European Commission, 2001).
2. The analysis by Balmaseda *et al.* (2000) also concludes that, in contrast with the United States, Spain did not benefit from a permanent supply shock during the recent period. This analysis, which is based on the estimate of a VAR model, shows that the sources of variations in GDP were essentially temporary shocks.
3. The estimate of the capital stock from investment data series, which incorporates computer software in accordance with the ESA95 methodology (European System of Accounts), is based on the assumption of a shorter life span (and thus a higher capital depreciation rate) over the recent period. This estimate, which is done by the OECD as for the other OECD countries, has only a slight effect on the final estimate of potential growth: if the capital stock had actually grown more rapidly, this would mean that the increase in capital productivity and thus in total factor productivity was smaller.

---

provide for pay catch-up clauses if inflation forecasts are exceeded. This is the consequence of the unpleasant price surprises of the last two years and the stalling of disinflation, which adversely affected agents' expectations.[16] These catch-up clauses were activated in 2000 and will be again in 2001. Thus the acceleration of wage settlements that took place between 1999 and 2000 continued at the beginning of 2001.[17] On balance, given the weak productivity growth, this has resulted in rising labour costs that have been passed on in producer prices since 1998 (Table 6, Panel A). Corporate profits, on the other hand, have been further squeezed as the

Table 6.   **Inflation decomposition: comparison between Spain and the euro area**
Percentage change

	Average 1994-98	1999	2000
A. Spain			
GDP deflator[1]	3.2	2.9	3.5
Labour cost[2]	2.9	3.4	4.1
Wages	3.3	3.0	4.2
Productivity	0.8	0.4	0.8
Employee ratio[3]	0.4	0.7	0.7
Net indirect taxes	5.2	8.8	4.2
Profits	3.2	0.8	2.4
Real wages	0.1	0.6	0.6
B. Euro area			
GDP deflator[1]	2.1	1.2	1.2
Labour cost[2]	1.2	1.4	1.2
Wages	2.4	1.7	2.0
Productivity	1.3	0.8	1.2
Employee ratio[3]	0.1	0.5	0.3
Net indirect taxes	4.6	4.0	0.4
Profits	2.6	0.1	1.6
Real wages	0.2	0.6	−0.1
C. Difference			
GDP deflator[1]	1.1	1.7	2.2
Labour cost[2]	1.7	1.9	3.0
Wages	0.9	1.3	2.2
Productivity	−0.5	−0.4	−0.4
Employee ratio[3]	0.3	0.2	0.3
Net indirect taxes	0.5	4.8	3.8
Profits	0.7	0.7	0.8
Real wages	0.0	0.0	0.7

1. The breakdown of inflation (measured by the GDP deflator) is obtained using the following accounting identity:

$$\frac{GDP}{GDP\ volume} = \frac{Total\ compensation\ of\ employees}{GDP\ volume} + \frac{Net\ indirect\ taxes}{GDP\ volume} + \frac{Profits}{GDP\ volume}$$

The first term represents the total labour cost in the economy, the second term represents the costs linked to net indirect taxes and the final term (defined as a residual of the identity) represents the contribution of profits and other revenues.
2. Wages less productivity plus the ratio of employees/total employment.
3. Ratio of employees to total employment.
Source: OECD calculations based on national accounts data.

result of an increase in net indirect taxation in 1999 and 2000 consistent with the buoyancy of revenue collected through this type of tax.

The rise in the consumer price index (CPI) continued to accelerate throughout 2000, reaching 4.0 per cent (year-on-year) in December. This compares with 2.9 per cent a year earlier and 1.4 per cent in December 1998. The oil price rise is partly responsible for this (Figure 7). The euro depreciation in 2000, which

Figure 7. **Consumer prices**
Percentage change

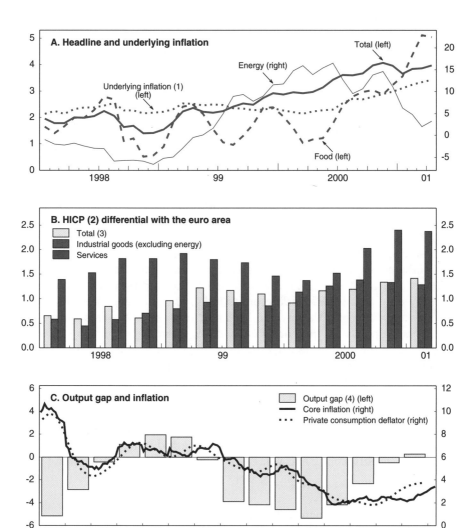

1. Excluding non-processed food and energy.
2. HICP: Harmonised Index of Consumer Prices.
3. Including energy and food; in 2000 inflation in these sectors performed relatively better in Spain than in the euro area.
4. As a per cent of potential GDP.
Source: INE, Ministry of Economy, Eurostat and OECD.

caused import prices to rise, was another factor, as were some special developments like the increase in certain food prices (*e.g.* pork, poultry). According to official estimates, the combination of these different factors increased inflation by 1½ percentage points in 2000, and is the main reason for the overshoot of the 2 per cent headline inflation target set for December of last year. Despite the recent easing of energy prices and the somewhat stronger euro, inflation was still close to 4 per cent in April 2001. The increase in inflation is not due solely to the special factors mentioned above. It also reflects the emergence of bottlenecks and the rise in unit labour costs. Underlying inflation, which had remained stable at around 2¼ per cent since 1998, accelerated as from the second quarter of 2000 and reached 3.4 per cent in April 2001. Capacity utilisation in industry in 2000 returned to a level similar to that in 1989-90, when the disinflation process that started in the late 1970s had come to a halt. The OECD's measure of the output gap, which turned slightly positive in 2000, would tend to confirm this.

The inflation differential between Spain and the rest of the euro area has been widening since 1998 and in the first quarter of 2001 showed a spread of 1¼ to 2½ points across various indicators: headline, underlying, service and industrial price inflation (Figure 7). Given that productivity growth is lower than in the other euro area countries, the differential's widening cannot be explained by convergence of the economy with its European neighbours[18] (Balassa-Samuelson model, see Blanchard, 2001). Indeed, the widening inflation gap between Spain and the rest of the euro area is due to differences in labour cost developments (Table 6, Panel C). Real wage growth between 1998 and 2000 was ½ percentage point per year higher in Spain than the euro area average, whereas productivity growth was nearly ½ percentage point lower. Moreover, in 1999 and 2000 net indirect taxes and corporate profits rose more rapidly in Spain than in the rest of the euro area. A detailed analysis of the movement of the consumer price index since 1996 also shows that prices in certain sectors (telephony, air transport and shipping) rose more steeply than in other EU countries (Alonso *et al.*, 2001). This may partly reflect a problem of CPI measurement, though this may also exist elsewhere. The method of calculating the price index was amended in January 2001 to correct some of the imperfections and will be reviewed again at the beginning of 2002 (Annex I).

A supportive macroeconomic policy led to strains in the economy

After Spain joined monetary union the main objective of economic policy was to maintain and prolong the present phase of expansion to keep employment rising rapidly and to accelerate the process of real convergence with the other EU countries. In this context, fiscal policy focussed on the continuing reduction and ultimate elimination of budget deficits (Figure 8). The authorities considered that this would open the way in the future for further tax cuts to stimulate the supply side

Figure 8. **General government budget**[1]
Per cent of GDP

1. OECD projections for 2001-02.
Source: INE and OECD.

Figure 9. **The macroeconomic policy stance**
Per cent

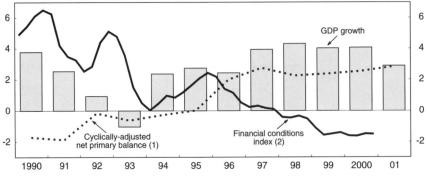

1. As a per cent of potential output.
2. The financial conditions indicator is computed as the weighted average of the real short-term and long-term interest
   rate and the real effective exchange rate (based on unit labour costs in manufacturing). The interest rate variable
   has a unitary coefficient while the exchange rate coefficient is the ratio of exports to GDP.
Source: OECD.

and would increase fiscal latitude for countering adverse shocks. The general government deficit was reduced from 3¼ per cent of GDP in 1997 to ¼ per cent in 2000 and a balanced budget should be attained in 2001, one year earlier than the target date set in the previous Stability Programme. This progress is due to both cyclical and structural factors.[19] The small reduction of the structural primary balance over the recent years indicates a slight tightening of the fiscal stance (Figure 9).

At the same time, monetary conditions, set at the euro area level, have been very easy for a country with higher growth and inflation rates than the euro area average. Credit growth has remained rapid and real interest rates are still low. The result has been a sharp rise in investment by corporations and households, whose saving ratio has declined. With demand growing faster than supply, partly reflecting increased private sector borrowing, production was slightly above potential in 2000. High capacity utilisation has been reflected in higher labour costs and inflation. This development has been more marked in the sheltered sector, notably construction, than in the exposed sector where profits have been squeezed because of increased competition. The current slowdown of activity might not be sufficient to reduce the inflationary pressures. If the trend continues it will restrain employment growth and risk affecting the growth momentum that Spain has enjoyed in recent years.

Deficit reduction since 1997 is attributable to cyclical and structural factors

The general government deficit dropped by nearly 3 percentage points of GDP between 1997 and 2000, with outcomes systematically better than the targets (Table 7 and Figure 10, Panel A). Efforts were also made to increase transparency and thus improve monitoring of the budget process. This has allowed a relatively good check on primary expenditure.[20] The authorities have also benefited from more favourable economic conditions than expected. Between 1997 and 2000 the economic growth assumptions used in setting the fiscal targets were on average more than ½ percentage point per year lower than the final outturns. Public deficit reduction was more marked than in the euro area on average,[21] the gross debt-to-GDP ratio declining by 7 percentage points between 1996 and 2000 (to 61 per cent of GDP) compared with an euro area average decline of 5 percentage points. The good fiscal performance was partly due to cyclical factors and the reduction of interest payments, which is of a structural nature.[22] Also the cyclically-adjusted primary balance contributed to some extent. The structural improvement in Spain's budget balance has been of the same order of magnitude as in the euro area countries since 1997 (Figure 10, Panel B).

The slowdown in fiscal consolidation since 1998 reflects the limits reached by the measures taken to date to hold down public expenditure. According to the

Table 7. **The fiscal consolidation process**

Per cent of potential GDP

| | 1995 | 1997 | 2000 | 2002[1] | Change over period | | |
					1995-97	1997-2000	2000-02[1]
Net lending	−6.6	−3.2	−0.3	0.1	3.4	2.9	0.4
Cyclical effects	−2.0	−1.7	0.2	0.2	0.3	1.9	0.0
Interest payments[2]	−4.6	−4.2	−3.1	−3.0	0.4	1.1	0.1
Structural primary balance	0.0	2.7	2.6	2.9	2.7	−0.1	0.3
of which:							
Structural revenues	37.0	37.6	38.1	38.4	0.6	0.5	0.3
Direct taxes	10.2	10.5	10.5	10.6	0.3	0.0	0.1
Indirect taxes	10.3	10.6	11.6	11.7	0.3	1.0	0.1
Social security contributions	12.9	13.0	13.4	13.5	0.1	0.4	0.1
Other revenues	3.6	3.5	2.6	2.6	−0.1	−0.9	0.0
Structural expenditure	37.0	35.0	35.6	35.6	−2.0	0.6	0.0
Consumption	17.3	16.9	16.9	16.6	−0.4	0.0	−0.3
Investment	3.6	3.0	3.3	3.5	−0.6	0.3	0.2
Social security expenditure	13.2	12.7	12.5	12.5	−0.5	−0.2	0.0
Other expenditure	2.9	2.4	2.9	3.0	−0.5	0.5	0.1

1. OECD projections.
2. The fall in interest payments can be included among the structural factors as it reflects the permanent elimination of risk premiums on interest rates due to the sounder economic conditions achieved prior to joining the euro area.
Source: OECD.

Figure 10. **The government deficit and the structural budget balance**
Per cent of GDP

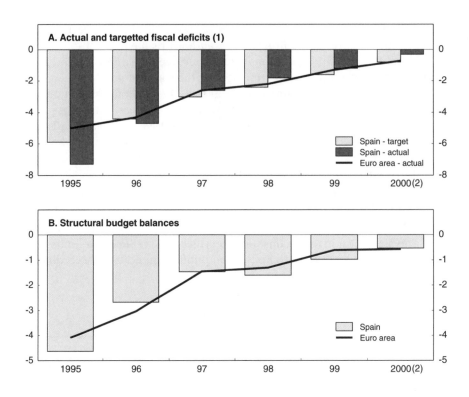

1. On the basis of SNA79 accounts for the period 1995-98.
2. Excluding UMTS proceeds.
Source: OECD.

OECD's calculations, structural primary expenditure as a proportion of GDP have increased in recent years, while they had declined in 1996 and 1997 (Table 7). The government consumption-to-potential GDP ratio remained stable despite the maintenance of restrictions on the replacement of retiring public servants that had been in place for several years, although it declined as a share of actual GDP. The regional governments appear to be having difficulty in complying with this constraint, perhaps because of their wider competencies due to the decentralisation process, and they have increasingly had recourse to temporary employment to meet their workforce requirements. Compared with other OECD countries, consumption expenditure as a percentage of GDP and the ratio of government employment to total employment are not yet high, however.[23] The ratio of public investment to output, which had declined in the early 90s, also rose as the authorities gave priority to the development of core infrastructure.[24] Finally, the reduction of other expenditure as a share of GDP, notably social transfers, has slowed since 1998 despite the continuing decline in unemployment. The factor chiefly responsible here has been the growth of pension expenditure. Pensions, which are inflation indexed, have undergone several discretionary increases and average pensions are rising faster than wages because of a particularly generous way of setting benefits (see Chapter III). Growth of primary expenditure was more than matched by growth of total revenue despite the 1999 personal income tax cuts, the latter's cost being estimated by the authorities at 0.5 per cent of GDP.[25] The favourable trend of activity and the 1999 income tax reform have broadened the tax base for the different taxes and contributions. The elasticity of tax revenues with respect to potential GDP has been particularly high for indirect taxes during the last few years, while the steep increases in the number of persons entering the social security system has boosted the growth of contributions.[26]

The 2000 and 2001 Budgets

In 2000, the general government deficit fell by 0.9 percentage point from its 1999 level and amounted to 0.3 per cent of GDP, this being ½ percentage point better than the initial target. The deficit of central government amounted to 0.7 per cent of GDP and that of regional and local government to 0.1 per cent, while the social security accounts showed a surplus of 0.5 per cent of GDP. As noted above, the greater-than-expected buoyancy of the economy largely accounts for these results. With output growth more than ½ percentage point above the budget forecast, the State's tax revenue was 0.5 per cent of GDP higher than projected. Most of this was due to the steeper-than-expected increase in receipts from personal income and corporation taxes, while revenue from indirect taxation was more or less on track. Receipts from social security contributions also increased more than expected owing to the continuing buoyancy of employment growth. A part of this revenue overshoot was used to finance expenditures that were higher than projected. This was especially the case with pensions, which rose significantly because of their linkage to the CPI. The 2 percentage point overshoot of the inflation target added ESP 355 billion (0.4 per cent of GDP) to pension expenditure. Half of this was financed from the 2000 Budget and half from the 2001 Budget. Other unforeseen expenditure items included compensation of haulage contractors and farmers for the energy price increase, although this was of a limited amount.

The 2001 Budget aims at balancing the general government account for the first time in 25 years. The central government deficit, which is officially projected at 0.3 per cent of GDP, will be offset by a projected surplus of the same size of the social security account, while the accounts of regional and local government should be in balance.[27] Furthermore, public debt is set to fall to below 60 per cent of GDP, the Maastricht debt criterion. This budget assumes real output growth of 3.6 per cent, which appears optimistic in the light of recent macroeconomic developments, although the official projection has been revised down to 3.2 per cent in April 2001. However, inflation could be well above the authorities' target of 2 per cent. For the first time in four years the government may have to forgo the benefit of higher-than-expected levels of activity. And the reduction of financial costs due to lower interest rates is likely to be less marked than in previous years. Even so, according to the OECD's projections, the balanced budget goal should be achieved in 2001. The projected improvement in the general government budget would be achieved essentially through an increase in the primary balance due to a slight decrease in expenditure as a percentage of GDP. Achieving the official target despite a less favourable environment is possible because the budget is built on cautious assumptions for revenues, especially from social security contributions.[28] Furthermore, the budget monitoring process has been strengthened this year to ensure that the balanced budget target will be achieved.[29]

On the revenue side the 2001 Budget shows no major change that would affect tax pressure significantly and no exceptional receipts from privatisation have been projected for this year (Table 8). Various tax cuts will be offset by commensurate increases. The excise taxes on tobacco, alcohol and fuels will continue to be frozen, as in 1999, and will not be adjusted upward for projected inflation. Small and medium-sized enterprises (SMEs) will benefit from a rate of corporation tax reduced from 35 to 30 per cent on the first ESP 15 million earned if their turnover does not exceed ESP 500 million (ESP 250 million previously). These businesses will also receive tax breaks for investment abroad and in new technologies and research and development (R&D). Measures to encourage saving have been introduced with a reduction of the capital gains tax from 20 to 18 per cent and a shortening of the minimum holding period to qualify for the reduced rate from two years to one year. The decrease in tax receipts resulting from these measures will be offset by a new tax on the use of the electromagnetic spectrum (applying mainly to third-generation mobile telephones), which should bring in revenue equivalent to 0.2 per cent of GDP. Non-indexation of personal income tax rates should slightly increase the tax pressure on households, which benefited from steep reductions in 1999 and 2000.

On the expenditure side, the 2001 Budget targets three priority areas. The first is social expenditure, with an increase of 7.3 per cent over the 2000 Budget which outpaces the projected 5.9 per cent growth of nominal GDP.[30] The fastest-growing items will be education (+9.6 per cent), family allowances (+13.1 per cent) and maternity benefits (+14.1 per cent). A further endowment for the social security reserve fund, amounting to ESP 90 billion or 0.1 per cent of GDP, is also budgeted. The second priority is investment in infrastructure, with an expenditure

Table 8. **General government accounts**

Per cent of GDP

	1996	1997	1998	1999	2000	2001[1]
Current receipts	37.4	37.7	37.8	38.2	38.4	38.5
Direct taxes	10.3	10.5	10.2	10.3	10.5	10.6
Household	8.2	7.7	7.5	7.0	6.9	6.9
Corporate	2.1	2.8	2.7	3.2	3.6	3.7
Indirect taxes	10.2	10.5	11.1	11.7	11.6	11.6
Social security contributions	13.2	13.1	13.1	13.1	13.4	13.4
Other	3.7	3.6	3.4	3.2	2.8	2.8
Current expenditure	38.6	37.3	36.6	35.5	34.9	34.6
Government consumption	17.5	17.2	17.2	16.9	16.8	16.6
of which: Wages and salaries	11.3	10.9	10.7	10.5	10.4	10.2
Subsidies	1.0	0.9	1.1	1.2	1.1	1.1
Social security outlays	13.8	13.3	12.8	12.4	12.4	12.4
Property income paid	5.3	4.8	4.3	3.6	3.3	3.2
Other	1.0	1.2	1.2	1.3	1.3	1.3
Saving	−1.2	0.4	1.2	2.8	3.4	3.8
Net capital outlays	3.7	3.6	3.8	4.0	3.8	3.9
Net lending	−4.9	−3.2	−2.6	−1.2	−0.3	0.0
Memorandum items						
Net primary balance[2]	0.0	1.2	1.4	2.2	2.7	3.0
Net borrowing of:						
Central government	−3.9	−2.7	−2.1	−1.1	−0.5	−0.3
Social security	−0.4	−0.2	−0.1	0.2	0.5	0.3
Local government	−0.6	−0.3	−0.3	−0.2	−0.3	0.0

1. Projections.
2. Difference between the actual balance and net interest payments.
Source: OECD and Ministry of Finance.

increase of 9.1 per cent over the 2000 Budget to develop the railways (high-speed trains), the road network and the water distribution system. The third priority area is investment in innovation and R&D, which is set to increase by 14.1 per cent. These spending increases will be offset by restraint on current outlays, notably on consumption, with a consequent reduction of the ratio of total public expenditure to GDP. Payroll expenditure will be restrained by a cap of 2 per cent on pay increases, in line with the government's inflation target, and maintenance of the restrictions on replacement of retiring public servants, although the effectiveness of this measure has diminished in recent years. Growth of labour market related spending will also be moderate; likewise the level of outlays on interest payments, although these may start to rise again in contrast to previous years. No specific provision has been made for the as yet hard-to-gauge budgetary impact of expenditure in connection with the bovine spongiform encephalopathy (mad cow disease) that has affected Spanish herds. However, the government plans to introduce a special tax to finance this, if necessary.

Assessment of fiscal policy in 2001

The decline in interest rates from which Spain benefited when entering the monetary union skewed its position relative to most other euro area countries. While, as measured by the structural deficit, fiscal policy did tighten since 1997, this has not significantly offset the easing of monetary conditions and fiscal policy slowed the momentum of the economy only a little. The improvement in the 2001 general government account will have a marginal damping effect on demand and by itself will not be sufficient to slow underlying inflation. Predicated on the official estimate of growth of 3.2 per cent, which is close to potential, the targeted reduction of the public deficit by ¼ point of GDP relative to 2000 will be essentially structural. Given an output gap that is positive in early 2001, a deceleration of activity would appear necessary. In any case, a slowdown is already under way. The scale of this fiscal tightening is small and in the case of a country like Spain, with its high foreign exposure, the budget multiplier is weak.[31] The stance of fiscal policy should therefore be carefully examined in the light of developments during the next months and notably as regards the international environment, which is still uncertain. Consistent also with long-term requirement, some further tightening of fiscal policy may be necessary. Although short-term fiscal policy is neither very effective nor very flexible for purposes of macroeconomic management, it is now the only one available to the authorities.

Challenges for fiscal policy in the medium term

Under Spain's new Stability Programme for the period 2000-04 – approved by the European Commission and Council in early 2001 – the general government balance could reach a surplus of 0.3 per cent of GDP by 2003 (Table 9). Both central government and the territorial administrations ought to be in balance as of 2003, while the social security account should maintain a surplus of ¼ per cent of GDP. A balanced general government budget could be achieved as of 2001 in Spain, which is earlier than the euro area average, but the surplus targeted for 2004 is similar to that of the other countries in the monetary union. The programme provides for a further reduction in the personal income tax, to take effect in 2003. This reform, the details of which have still to be spelled out, will not jeopardise fiscal prudence.[32] This is because the plan includes a reduction in total public spending as a proportion of GDP, to be achieved by further cuts in current expenditure. Capital spending, on the other hand, is budgeted to continue to grow briskly. Lastly, the Stability Programme contains measures to enhance the financial viability of the social security system. To this end, the surpluses of the

Table 9. **Stability Programme 2000-04**[1]

	Annual average percentage growth			
	1999	2000	2001	Average 2002-04
Macroeconomic scenario				
Real GDP growth[2]	4.0	4.0	3.6	3.2
Private consumption[3]	4.7	4.0	3.4	2.8
Government consumption	2.9	1.2	1.2	1.8
Gross fixed capital formation	8.9	7.0	7.0	5.3
External sector[2, 4]	−1.5	−0.4	−0.4	−0.1
Private consumption deflator	2.5	3.2	2.7	2.0
Employment[5]	3.6	3.0	2.5	2.1

	Per cent of GDP					
	1999	2000	2001	2002	2003	2004
General government accounts[6]						
Primary balance	2.5	3.0	3.3	3.4	3.5	3.5
Total revenues	40.0	40.4	40.6	40.6	40.4	40.3
Total expenditure	41.1	40.7	40.6	40.4	40.1	40.0
Current expenditure	35.8	35.4	35.1	34.8	34.4	34.2
of which: Interest payments	3.6	3.3	3.3	3.2	3.2	3.2
Capital expenditure	5.3	5.4	5.5	5.6	5.7	5.7
General government deficit (−) or surplus (+)	−1.1	−0.3	0.0	0.2	0.3	0.3
State[7]	−1.1	−0.7	−0.3	−0.1	0.0	0.0
Social security	0.2	0.5	0.3	0.3	0.3	0.3
Territorial governments	−0.2	−0.1	0.0	0.0	0.0	0.0
Gross debt	63.3	61.1	58.9	56.6	52.8	49.6
Memorandum item General government deficit (−) or surplus (+) Euro area average	−1.3	−0.8	−0.7	−0.3	0.0	0.4

1. Data for 1999 are provisional, data for 2000 onwards are projections.
2. Constant 1995 prices.
3. Households and non-profit institutions serving households.
4. Contribution to GDP growth.
5. Full-time equivalent jobs.
6. On a national accounts basis.
7. Including Autonomous Agencies.
Source: Ministry of Economy (2001), "Stability Programme Update" and European Commission.

social security system will probably be used to increase the transfers to the social security reserve fund whose accumulated resources will reach 1 per cent of GDP in 2004. The reduction in general government debt, which could amount to 10 per cent of GDP between 2000 and 2004, will also have the effect of limiting transfers detrimental to future generations.

There are two main threats to the implementation of the Stability Programme. The first concerns the macroeconomic framework on which it is based. The assumption that activity will continue to expand at a rate of 3.2 per cent per year up until 2004, while inflation remains stable at 2 per cent, seems optimistic. The economy's growth potential could well turn out to be below 3 per cent over the next few years, even assuming a continuing fall in structural unemployment, if productivity growth does not accelerate substantially. The sensitivity tests conducted by the government suggest, however, that general government financial equilibrium will be maintained if the expansion of activity is restricted to 2.7 per cent on average between 2002 and 2004. On the other hand, the planned tax cuts and/or the increase in funding of the social security reserve would no doubt be in jeopardy. A second less important risk is the possibility of the government being obliged to award civil servants a wage catch-up following a recent decision by the National Court (Audiencía Nacional) to end the freeze on compensation imposed in 1997. The implementation of this court order was suspended following a government appeal lodged with the Constitutional Court, emphasising that the budget incorporating the freeze had been passed by Parliament.[33] If the decision were to be confirmed, however, the cost to the public finances could be the equivalent of between 0.3 and 0.4 per cent of GDP.[34]

Given the macroeconomic assumptions, the fiscal target adopted by the authorities in their Stability Programme would appear to be of little ambition, bearing in mind the challenges that the Spanish economy will have to meet in the medium and long term. Keeping a balanced budget is necessary in order to have sufficient leeway to allow the automatic stabilisers to work freely in the event of a shock affecting the economy, or indeed to act in a discretionary manner in the event of a serious disturbance, while at the same time abiding by the Stability and Growth Pact.[35] However, a higher fiscal surplus is likely to be necessary in the medium term in order to respect the constraints which would be imposed by the new fiscal stability law if it is adopted (see below). On the other hand, further reduction in household taxation is desirable as a way of encouraging individual initiative and promoting work, bearing in mind the low employment ratio. Similarly, the priority being attached to infrastructure development is welcome because it is likely to promote a better nexus between the regions and thereby ease the problems deriving from their differences in efficiency and resources, which are themselves liable to curb potential output growth.These objectives will not, however, be compatible over the medium and long term unless the authorities can keep effective control over other outlays. Considerable efforts have already been made with regard to payroll costs. While further efficiency gains can no doubt still be made, in particular by making increased use of new technologies, it is probably going to prove increasingly difficult to squeeze this sort of expenditure any more in the future, especially as it is important to keep civil service pay at a level that will continue to attract skilled and enthusiastic staff. That said, progress is needed as regards administrative reform and employment management in the public sector, the aim being to encourage increased human resource mobility and more modern management methods. Also, further steps must be taken, as a matter of priority, in order to better control social expenditure, in particular pensions and certain forms of health spending such as drug consumption, which is where the greatest pressure will be felt in the future. Where pensions are concerned, the increase in reserve fund resources and the continuing reduction in central government debt are no doubt part of the answer to the problems posed by ageing but not, by any means, a sufficient response (see Chapter III).

The fiscal stability law

In conjunction with the preparation of the 2001 Budget and the Stability Programme, the authorities drew up a draft fiscal stability law, the aim of which is to abandon deficit financing as one way of financing public expenditure and to ensure that, in future, government accounts balance or show a surplus. Given the highly decentralised nature of Spain, the draft law seeks to impose balanced budgets at all levels of government: central, social, territorial and local, as well as public enterprises and corporations. Each level of government will be free to decide whether this objective should be achieved by increasing revenue or cutting expenditure. The possibility of running deficits will not be ruled out, but will be restricted to temporary and exceptional situations and have to be duly justified. In this event, plans to restore the accounts to balance will have to be presented. These plans, covering a period of 2 to 3 years, will be discussed in Parliament. The balanced budget rule will be implemented along with three other principles: multi-annual targets, transparency and efficiency.[36] The law, which will be implemented for the first time in the 2003 Budget, will be set within a multi-annual framework. At the start of each year, the government will set three-year overall fiscal stability targets for all government levels. Once they have been discussed and approved by Parliament, the budgets of the various authorities will then be drawn up. The Council for co-ordination of regional fiscal policies (*Consejo de Política Fiscal y Financiera*), a body comprising the ministers for economic affairs and the budget and representatives of each Autonomous Community, will be responsible for co-ordinating fiscal policy at the level of each Community to ensure consistency with these broad objectives.[37] Compliance with these objectives by each entity will be checked by developing a statistical information system, which will permit greater transparency and more effective monitoring of regional government accounts.[38] In the event of non-compliance with these objectives by the Communities, their borrowing capacity (and thus that of the bodies dependent on them) could be curbed by the central government, which would have to authorise deficits. Penalties may also be imposed.[39] Lastly, the draft law introduces two innovations that will affect the central government fiscal process: firstly, a cap will be put on expenditure within the framework of multi-annual scenarios voted by Parliament at the start of each year; and secondly, a contingency fund (representing 2 per cent of expenditure) will be set up to cover unscheduled expenditure.[40]

The decision to implement this draft law reflects the authorities' resolve to maintain the fiscal discipline needed to ensure that Spain's favourable performance in the past five years continues. It strengthens fiscal discipline at a timely moment, since that discipline is not as firmly entrenched in Spain as in some other OECD countries,[41] while the cycle's positive effect on public finance tends to encourage increased spending and tax cuts. The improvement in the information concerning budget out-turns, which the law provides for, and the increased obligation of transparency at all levels of government, are steps in the right direction. This draft law is much more binding than the rule imposed by the Stability and Growth Pact. It partly draws upon the European Council's recommendations of June 2000 in Santa Maria de Feira, which urged Member State governments to pursue fiscal consolidation beyond the mini-mum required by the Stability Pact. By obliging social security to ensure that its accounts are permanently balanced, the law, if approved, should in principle prompt the government to implement the reforms needed to address the pressures put on pensions by population ageing. Similarly, the Communities, which are responsible for managing social and health care expenditure, will also have to take steps to deal with the problems posed by rising expenditure.[42] By requiring that the budgets of all lev-els of government be balanced in *all periods*, the draft law seems however to exclude implicitly the possibility of accumulating assets now and spending them through defi-cits in the future to deal with the consequences of population ageing.[43] Nevertheless, the implementation of this draft law should lead to a decline in public debt.

While many aspects of the fiscal stability draft law seem positive, it does nevertheless contain several risks. For example, it is important to ensure that the framework does not excessively limit fiscal policy, which remains the sole tool available for dealing in the short term with an asymmetric shock. A similar ques-tion arises at the lower levels of government, which can be affected by asymmetric shocks too. The obligation to maintain a balanced budget at all levels of govern-ment may make it necessary to maintain a substantial budget surplus perma-nently in order to cope with cyclical variations. Flexibility will depend on what is meant by an "exceptional situation" in the draft law, which is not explicit on this point. In particular, it is not specified whether recessions will be considered exceptional situations since the draft law confines itself to general principles.[44] The law could also pose difficulties for local governments if they do not have suffi-ciently stable resources. Currently, the regions have the guarantee that their reve-nue will increase by at least the same rate as nominal GDP. Discussions have begun recently concerning the reform of the system of financing the Communities, which expires at end-2001 (Chapter II). The reform of the financing system will therefore have to address this problem so that the fiscal stability law can be applied to local governments without major difficulties.

Prospects

The OECD's projections (Table 10) suggest that the slowdown in domestic demand and a flagging external environment will probably bring the growth of

Table 10.   **Short-term prospects**

Percentage change[1]

	1999	2000	2001	2002
Private consumption	4.7	4.0	2.9	2.9
Government consumption	2.9	2.6	2.3	1.7
Gross fixed investment	8.9	5.9	4.1	3.9
Total domestic demand	5.5	4.1	2.9	2.9
Exports of goods and services	6.6	10.8	8.2	7.4
Imports of goods and services	11.9	10.4	8.0	7.3
Foreign balance[2]	−1.5	−0.1	−0.1	−0.1
Gross domestic product	4.0	4.1	2.9	2.9
Household saving ratio[3]	12.0	11.6	12.1	12.3
Employment[4]	4.6	4.8	2.9	2.2
Unemployment rate (%)	15.9	14.1	13.2	12.6
Private consumption deflator	2.4	3.6	3.2	2.8
GDP deflator	2.9	3.5	3.5	3.0
Wage rate, total economy	3.0	4.2	4.1	4.2
Unit labour cost, total economy	3.4	4.1	3.6	3.2
Output gap (%)[5]	−0.5	0.3	0.3	0.4
As a % of GDP:				
Current account balance	−2.1	−3.1	−3.2	−3.2
Net lending of government	−1.2	−0.3	0.0	0.1
Primary government balance	2.2	2.7	3.0	3.0

1. Constant prices for GDP and its components.
2. Contribution to growth of GDP.
3. Household saving as a percentage of disposable income.
4. Labour force survey definition.
5. Deviations of actual GDP from potential GDP as a percentage of potential GDP.
Source: OECD.

activity down to a more sustainable rate of some 3 per cent in 2001 and 2002. With fiscal policy tightening slightly, household consumption is likely to moderate and the saving ratio to pick up a little, thus prolonging the deceleration seen in the second half of 2000. The decline in consumer confidence caused by the financial market downturn and uncertainty as to how the international environment is going to evolve could prompt households, whose financial capacity has diminished appreciably in recent years, to limit the growth of their purchases. Even so, consumption growth should be underpinned by a continuing brisk rise in disposable income, with real wages affected by wage indexation in the wake of the oil shock and vigorous job creation persisting. Investment is also likely to ease, reflecting caution on the part of firms, prompted by the uncertainty as to how economic conditions are likely to develop. A number of factors ought, however, to limit the deceleration in the growth of capital expenditure. With the authorities launching infrastructure development projects, public investment is set to expand rapidly and low real interest rates should continue to favour residential investment. Corporate profitability still looks favourable despite margins being reduced in the exposed sector, while pressure on capacity remains high. With domestic demand less buoyant, the rate of growth of imports is likely to ease. The slowdown in external demand following the deceleration of the US economy, plus the decline in competitiveness due to the stronger euro, should curb export growth, with the result that the contribution of foreign trade to activity may remain close to zero. Bearing in mind, too, the improvement in the terms of trade stemming from the fall in energy prices, the current account deficit should stabilise around 3¼ per cent of GDP.

A slowdown in demand to a rate similar to that of potential output should help to ease pressure on capacity somewhat, while the fall in energy prices and the somewhat stronger euro will restrain import prices. Inflation could thus come down to around 3 per cent on average in 2001 and 2002, while underlying inflation should stabilise, as should the inflation differential vis-à-vis the other euro area countries. Employment growth, although more moderate than in previous years, ought to further reduce unemployment to some 12½ per cent by 2002. The upward pressure on the labour market stemming from the reduced number of job-seekers, coupled with the wage catch-up resulting from the indexation clauses being activated by the surge in inflation in 2000, will probably cause a further moderate acceleration in workers' compensation. The increase in unit labour costs could, however, slow a little thanks to somewhat stronger productivity gains, which should help to check the squeeze on corporate profit margins.

The main domestic risk to this scenario concerns the trend in wages. If future settlements incorporate the hike in inflationary expectations prompted by poor inflation outcomes in 2000 and the indexation mechanisms already in place, competitiveness would be harmed and the continued buoyancy of job creation would be undermined. A surge in inflation, coupled with persisting stock market instability and unfavourable developments on the external side, could do serious damage to household and business confidence. The slowdown in domestic demand observed in late 2000 could, in that case, continue into 2001 and the economy could experience a harder landing.

II.   Reform options to boost sustainable growth

The strong output and employment growth of recent years has not been accompanied by an improved productivity performance. Multi-factor productivity growth has been lower in the 90s than during the 80s and is low in international comparison (Figure 11). As a result, the growth of potential output has not picked up (Chapter I). Labour productivity has actually decelerated in the second half of the 90s, largely reflecting strong job creation, with many unskilled workers entering the labour market. In other countries, such as the United States, Ireland, Finland or Sweden strong productivity growth has gone hand in hand with strong employment creation. In these countries high-technology sectors have played an important role in boosting potential. In Spain, however, the "new" economy has so far not had a visible impact on aggregate outcomes (Box 3).

Figure 11.   **Total factor productivity growth**[1]
Average growth over period, per cent

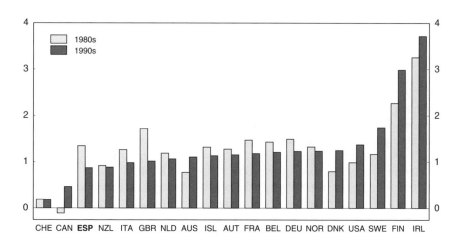

1. Trend.
Source: OECD.

Box 3.   Has the "new economy" arrived in Spain?

Aggregate indicators of productivity and the use of information and communication technology (ICT) reveal that the strong growth performance in recent years has not been the consequence of the emergence of the "new economy". "New economy" indicators show that expenditure on ICT is under 2 per cent of GDP, far below the OECD average of over 4 per cent (OECD, 2000b). Although the liberalisation of telecommunications has gained momentum, prices of fixed telephony are still above the OECD average, thus inhibiting the use of the Internet. Spain is also lagging in terms of Internet subscribers (9.2 per 100 inhabitants compared with an average of 10.9 for the OECD as of January 2000) and especially in Internet hosts (15.7 per 100 inhabitants against 37.4 for the OECD) while the use of electronic commerce is still in its infancy. Overall R&D expenditures have decreased over the 90s, and were in 1999 less than 0.5 per cent of GDP, much lower than the OECD average of 2 per cent. In some specific sectors, though, new economy features have emerged. Internet banking, for example, has been developed very quickly, and all major banks have created their own Internet subsidiaries in which they have invested heavily. But the spread of the use of new technologies in a wide range of areas, which would lead to a deep impact of the new economy on macroeconomic activity, has not taken place yet (Fundación Cotec, 2000). However, the potential gains from the emergence of a new economy should be quite large, given the low starting point. A recent study (BBVA, 2000) finds that the potential increase in annual GDP growth could be 0.7 per cent over the next ten years if the necessary reforms are implemented.

The Spanish authorities are aware of these shortcomings, and have made efforts to promote the new economy in a special ICT plan, Info XXI, which includes funding of ESP 825 billion between 2001 and 2003, almost twice as much as in the previous budgets. The plan includes many measures, such as a high speed Internet link for all schools, a special Internet network for researchers, and the generalisation of the use of the Internet between the public administration and the general public. On top of that, R&D and ICT investment is promoted through generous tax credits in the corporate tax, while the emergence of small and dynamic firms has been favoured by a new venture capital law in 1998.

On the other hand, the considerable reform efforts of the Spanish authorities should have lifted productivity in the "old" economy. The government is aware of the importance of regulatory reform in the present context and has implemented a comprehensive package of measures through a set of Royal Decrees (March and October 1999, and June 2000). These measures aim at accelerating and improving the liberalisation process in some key product markets. Some of these measures have already produced a direct effect in terms of lower prices and boosting output (especially in the telecommunications sector), while in others a longer period is needed to yield visible effects. The privatisation programme has been extensive and only a few large companies remain in public hands (the railways, the post office – which has still a monopoly for some services, coal mining and shipbuilding companies, sea ports and the national and regional public television channels). Privatisation in key sectors has gone together with liberalisation, leading to greater competitive pressures. In tele-communications, *Telefónica* (the incumbent operator) competes now with three companies in fixed telephony and with two in mobile telephony; and in electricity and natural gas distribution full liberalisation has been brought forward. Also in other sectors, barriers have been brought down, and the competition and regulatory bodies have promoted competition. The government approved another ambitious liberalisation package in June 2000 (Annex II) that further liberalises a wide range of areas, and prevents additional concentration in network industries. In the labour market, the introduction of permanent contracts with lower severance payments for some workers in 1997 has been followed by new measures in the same direction in 2001, although they have been accompanied by increased firing costs for temporary work. In financial markets, substantial changes were introduced in 1999 to promote venture capital, while the reform of the stock market law in 1998 introduced greater investment opportunities for mutual funds. Other reforms, focusing on the public sector, have been announced. The government is committed to reform the corporate tax and to further reduce the personal income tax in 2003. At the same time, the decentralisation of competencies to the Autonomous Communities (as regions are called) has regained momentum recently, whereas the financing system of the regions will be revamped.

Weak productivity growth in recent years could be attributed to some extent to the share of new jobs that have been filled by less skilled workers. As these workers acquire work experience, productivity growth should recover even though this is likely to be a slow process. In the meantime, to ensure more rapid convergence with high-income countries, reform efforts must continue to strengthen the potential growth of the economy. The labour market still presents many rigidities, especially when compared to those OECD countries with low unemployment. In particular, employment protection legislation (EPL) is still very restrictive, while wage bargaining is in need of deep changes to avoid competitiveness losses, which might be difficult to regain quickly in the euro area. Active labour market policies (ALMP) must become more effective and focus on raising the skills of those entering the labour market. In product markets, the authorities must stay vigilant to ensure that high levels of concentration in some key sectors (like electricity, oil and gas distribution, airlines and mobile telephony) are not abused to restrict competition. As shown in the OECD's 2000 Review of *Regulatory Reform in Spain* (OECD, 2000c), there are many ways to enhance the regulatory framework, which have only been partly implemented, and there is still considerable scope for further price reductions in key sectors. Independent regulators should play a major role in enhancing competition, and they should be provided with sufficient powers and resources to do their job properly. In many areas, the role of Autonomous Communities is increasingly important, and new powers should not be used to undermine reform efforts at the national level, be it in retail distribution, land development, or through the proliferation of regional public enterprises. This chapter reviews these various structural issues dealing with labour, product and financial markets as well as public sector issues with a synopsis of the OECD's recommendations for structural reform being provided in Table 11.

Table 11. **Recommendations for further structural reform**

Based on previous and current *Surveys* and action taken since early 2000

Previous Survey	Action taken	Current Survey
LABOUR MARKET		
A. Reform employment protection provisions		
Undertake comprehensive reform of employment protection legislation encompassing core workers.	Permanent contracts with lower severance payments have been extended to new groups of workers. New firing costs implemented for temporary workers.[1]	Reduce the gap in severance payments between permanent and temporary workers by reducing protection for core workers.
Ensure decisions of the labour courts concerning severance payments conform to the spirit of existing legislation.		Same as previous *Survey*.
Eliminate administrative approval for collective dismissals.		Same as previous *Survey*.
Streamline existing incentives to use permanent contracts through lower social security contributions, to minimise displacement effects.	Incentives have been suppressed for most temporary workers, and increased for other groups.	No further action required.
B. Reform unemployment benefit system		
Ensure that job search incentives are not affected by the extension of unemployment coverage to long-term unemployed aged over 45.		Same as previous *Survey*.
Consider taking into account severance payments when compensating unemployed for loss of a job.		Same as previous *Survey*.
Restrict eligibility conditions of the unemployment subsidy programme for the rural sector to enhance regional labour mobility.		Same as previous *Survey*.
C. Increase labour cost and working-time flexibility		
Reach an agreement on the suppression of sector and provincial levels of wage deals to enhance wage flexibility, firms' competitiveness and the regional mobility of labour.		Same as previous *Survey*. Substitute the automatic application of a sectoral agreement in each firm by an "opt-in" clause.

Table 11. **Recommendations for further structural reform** (*cont.*)
Based on previous and current *Surveys* and action taken since early 2000

Previous Survey	Action taken	Current Survey
Lift social security contribution ceilings to reduce labour costs of the low paid.		Same as previous Survey.
Improve the flexibility of the new part-time permanent work contract.	Wider definition of part-time work and more flexible arrangements for distribution of hours.	Monitor the effectiveness of the reform.
Discourage regional initiatives to reduce working time since they raise labour costs and impede employment gains.		Same as previous Survey.
D. Enhance active labour market policies		
Unemployment benefits should be linked to training and/or workfare.		Same as previous Survey.
Enhance monitoring of the effectiveness of active labour market programmes.		Same as previous Survey.
Training programmes should maximise work experience.		Same as previous Survey.
PRODUCT MARKETS		
A. Enhance product market competition		
Implement the competition law rapidly. Consider merging the *Tribunal* and the *Servicio de la Defensa de la Competencia* to set up a single independent competition authority.	The law was approved in December 1999. Mergers cannot go through until competition authorities have approved them.	Increase the resources of the Competition Authorities and consider consolidating decision processes. Ensure that regional competition tribunals do not add substantially to costs of competition policy.
Introduce more rational pricing for water and consider extending the market of property rights for all water resources.	A new National Water Plan has been approved that projects investments equivalent to 4% of GDP in 8 years. A large water transfer project is planned for the east of the country.	Use higher prices to restrict water demand, ensuring that the price of water reflects all costs (economic and environmental) before making water transfers.
Simplify the criteria and reduce the waiting period for obtaining building permits.	Denying a permit to develop land will require a justification from municipalities. No response from the authorities will be considered as a tacit approval.	Deeper reforms are needed.
Further liberalise postal services.		Same as previous Survey.
Open rail transport to competition and consider franchising in railways and urban transport.	Current plans for liberalisation of long distance passenger transport in 2002.	Ensure that liberalisation plans are implemented rapidly.

Table 11. **Recommendations for further structural reform** (*cont.*)
Based on previous and current *Surveys* and action taken since early 2000

Previous Survey	Action taken	Current Survey
Enhance competition in electricity generation and promote competition in the gas sector. Review the effects of cross-ownership in both markets to avoid anti-competitive conduct.	Liberalisation calendar brought forward: full choice of provider to 2003 for electricity and gas. Growth limitations for the two largest electricity generators during 5 and 3 years, respectively.	Envisage splitting up the large electricity generators. Separate electricity generation from distribution. Study the options to import electricity.
	Capital of the wholesale gas distributor opened to competitors.	Allow competitors to build their own retail network in gas distribution before the current deadline.
Improve transparency in the setting of telecommunication charges and streamline procedures and conditions to obtain a licence.	Access to the local loop of Telefónica opened to competitors. Lump-sum tax for Internet at non-peak hours.	Increase powers of the sectoral regulator (CMT). Ensure that access tariffs respond to long-term incremental costs.
	Four UMTS licences awarded through a beauty contest. Increase in the tax on the electromagnetic spectrum. Two more GSM licences to be awarded.	Define a framework conducive to investment in mobile telephony.
Reduce regions' restrictions on shop-opening hours for retail trade.	The maximum number of opening hours per week has been raised from 72 to 90. Opening Sundays raised from 8 to 12 per year. For outlets with a surface of less than 300 square metres, opening and business hours have been fully liberalised.	Autonomous communities should not restrain the establishment of new hypermarkets in their territories.
Reduce further the administrative steps necessary to create a new business.		Same as previous *Survey*.
B. Public subsidies		
Lower public support to industry and concentrate on horizontal targets to prevent distortions to competition.		Same as previous *Survey*.
Focus national support to agriculture more on restructuring incentives and promote transparency in the distribution of subsidies by the State and the regions.		Same as previous *Survey*.

Table 11. **Recommendations for further structural reform** (*cont.*)

Based on previous and current *Surveys* and action taken since early 2000

Previous *Survey*	Action taken	Current *Survey*
FINANCIAL MARKETS		
Stay vigilant on prudential banking supervision and on risk management practices of large credit institutions.	Risk management regulations have been enhanced to adapt them better to the business cycle.	Remain vigilant on prudential banking supervision.
Ensure a level playing field in banking and promote ownership forms for savings banks that allow market-driven restructuring of the banking system.		Same as previous *Survey*. Ensure political interests do not interfere with the management of savings banks. Promote consolidation of small savings banks.
PUBLIC SECTOR		
Speed up implementation of hospital management reforms and adopt global budgets instead of line budgeting for the remaining ones.		Same as previous *Survey*.
Extend and speed up the authorisation of generics while introducing a co-payment on pharmaceuticals for pensioners.		Same as previous *Survey*.
Improve incentives for geographic mobility of civil servants to match increasing devolution of spending powers to regions by corresponding shifts in public employment.		Same as previous *Survey*. Develop a new financing system for regions that promotes fiscal responsibility of autonomous communities.

1. Before 2001, collective agreements in some sectors had already included severance payments for temporary workers.

Source: OECD.

Labour market reforms

Labour market performance has been remarkable in recent years. Job creation, as measured by the national accounts, averaged 3.5 per cent since 1997,[45] while the unemployment rate decreased rapidly from over 20 to 13.6 per cent at the end of 2000. The unemployment rate is, however, still the highest in the OECD area and the labour market is still characterised by a low participation rate, a very high proportion of temporary contracts and a low share of part-time work (Figures 12 and 13). These features concern the young and women most, who also suffer more under high unemployment than adult men (Figure 14). To some extent these characteristics are due to historical and cultural factors (like the low incidence of part-time work or the low participation rate of women), but labour market distortions also play a key role. Despite the reduction of severance payments due to the 1997 labour market reform, employment protection legislation for core workers is still very rigid, and adds substantially to labour costs for workers on permanent contracts. At the same time, wage bargaining is not flexible enough to allow for wage differentials to reflect firm-level productivity differentials. New measures taken in early 2001 have broadened the 1997 reform measures and have made part-time work more flexible, but they have also introduced restrictions on

Figure 12. **Temporary employment contracts by sector**
Per cent of total contracts in the same sector

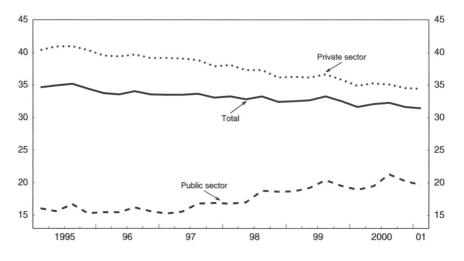

Source: INE (Labour Force Survey) and Ministry of Economy.

Figure 13.   **Part-time employment in international perspective**
As a per cent of total employment, 1999

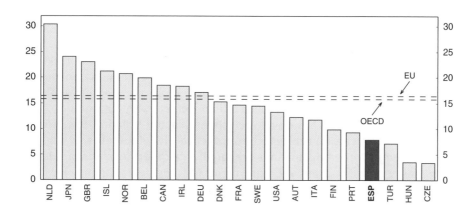

1. Part-time employment refers to persons who usually work less than 30 hours per week in their main job. For Japan
    less than 35 hours per week. Data include only persons declaring usual hours except for Finland and Japan where
    data are based on actual hours worked. For the United States, data are for wage and salary earners only.
    Source: OECD (2000), *Employment Outlook.*

Figure 14.   **Incidence of unemployment by age and sex**
Per cent

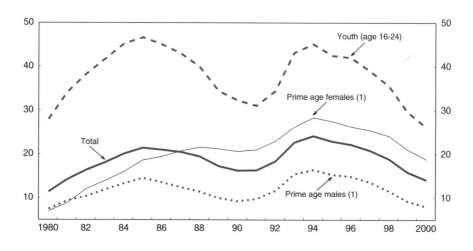

1. Age 25 to 54.
Source: INE (Labour Force Survey) and Ministry of Economy.

temporary employment (which already existed in some sectors[46]) and have not made progress in reducing the overall level of EPL or in reforming the wage bargaining system.

Employment protection remains high

Very strict EPL was inherited from the Franco regime, and the difficulties it posed for employment creation after the oil crises in the 1970s prompted the liberalisation of temporary contracts in 1984. The share of such contracts has increased rapidly since then, though most of the employment adjustment during the deep recession of the early 90s also fell on workers with temporary contracts. A three-tier labour market has developed (Bentolila and Dolado, 1994), with permanent workers (insiders) protected from cyclical developments by high firing costs, while employment fluctuations are largely absorbed by shifts of temporary workers between working and unemployment. This segmentation may have negative consequences. High use of temporary work may have negative effects on human capital formation (OECD, 2000d) and thus may explain part of the sluggish productivity performance. It may also partly explain the low rate of outward migration from high unemployment areas, as very short (usually three or six month) contracts do not provide a sufficient incentive to counterbalance the substantial fixed costs of geographic mobility, although cultural factors are also important in this respect.[47] The distorting effects of the stringent EPL have been evident in Spain for many years, and led to reform initiatives in 1994 and 1997, and further measures were approved in March 2001. However, despite some positive effects on employment creation, these reforms have not reduced the stringency of EPL for core workers much so far.

The main goal of the 1997 labour market reform was to encourage new permanent jobs, thus reducing the share of temporary contracts in the economy. The central element was a new permanent contract with lower firing costs for those groups with special difficulties in entering permanent jobs (Table 12). In addition, the government supported these contracts with reductions in social security contributions of between 20 and 60 per cent for two years, depending on the targeted group. These subsidies have been modified and prolonged subsequently, while also broadening the coverage to those groups for which the reform was less successful.

The reform worked very well in creating permanent employment (more than 2.5 million new-type contracts were signed between 1997 and 2000), although it is difficult to disentangle the factors that have led to this increase. On the one hand, the reduction of severance payments for new indefinite contracts has lowered long-term labour costs, and has therefore reduced the barrier to hire workers permanently. Furthermore, lower social security contributions were probably an instrument at least as powerful as that of lower firing costs, since the average

Table 12.   **EPL: severance payments**

	Temporary contracts[1]	Permanent contracts	
		Justified dismissals	Unjustified dismissals
Spain, before and after the reform (days of salary per year worked)			
Before 1997	0	33	45
Reform 1997			
Special groups[2]	0	20	33
Others	0	33	45
Reform 2001			
Special groups[3]	8	20	33
Others	8	33	45

	Justified dismissals after			Unjustified dismissals after 20 years
	9 months	4 years	20 years	
For permanent contracts in several OECD countries (months of salary)				
Spain				
Special groups[2]	0.5	2.6	12	22
Others	0.8	4.1	12	30
France	0	0.4	2.7	15
Germany	0	0	0	18
Italy	0.7	3.5	18	32.5
United Kingdom	0	0	0	0
Canada	0	0.3	1.3	Disparate rulings
Japan	0	1.5	4	26
United States	0	0	0	Disparate rulings

1. Before 2001, collective agreements in some sectors had already included severance payments for temporary workers.
2. Long-term unemployed (over one year), temporary workers, young workers (aged 18-30), older workers (aged over 45) and women in special sectors.
3. Long-term unemployed (over 6 months), temporary workers, young workers (aged 16-30), older workers (aged over 45), women in sectors with a lower employment ratio and disabled workers.
Source: OECD (1999), *Employment Outlook* and OECD calculations.

reduction of 40 per cent in social charges implies a considerable temporary fall of the cost of permanent work (of about 12 per cent of total labour cost per year). On the other hand, the increase in temporary contracts has also been impressive and the share of temporary contracts has barely changed, although there has been some reduction of temporary employment in the private sector compensated by an increase in the public sector.[48] Indeed, strong job creation in both the permanent and the temporary segments of the market suggests that the remarkable labour market performance owes more to exceptionally strong cyclical labour demand rather than to the incentives introduced by the reform, although it is likely that without the reform the share of temporary contracts would have risen beyond the current level.

The 1997 agreement was valid for four years, and will expire in May 2001. Given strong job creation, and in view of the persistence of a large share of temporary work, the government encouraged the social partners to negotiate a deepening of the reform. Since the social partners could not come to an agreement after six months of discussions, the government approved new measures on EPL, together with other labour market measures (Annex III). Firing costs have been introduced for temporary contracts, while the permanent contract with lower severance payments approved in 1997 has been prolonged beyond 2001, and its coverage has been extended. Male workers between 30 and 45 years are now the only group remaining on the old contract. On the contrary, lower social security contributions will apply now to all newly signed indefinite contracts.

The recent reform initiative may help to reduce the share of temporary work by closing the gap in firing costs between permanent and temporary work; but it does move in the wrong direction as it increases firing costs for fixed-term employment in those sectors where they did not exist[49] and barely reduces them for open-ended contracts. New severance payments for fixed-term contracts add to higher social security contributions for temporary work which were already approved in 1999 (of 0.5 per cent in general, and of 1.5 per cent if the work is carried out by a temporary work agency). Overall, the stringency of EPL remains among the highest in the OECD, and has changed little with respect to 1997 as restrictions on fixed-term contracts are not compensated by a significantly lower EPL for the new permanent contracts (Table 12). Moreover, the labour market could become even more fragmented. This fragmentation creates inequities among workers without reducing the bargaining power of core workers (those with high protection) and the reform may have some detrimental effects on future job creation.

Several options for further reform are available. *First*, firms and workers could determine the level of severance payments in their wage contracts. This would introduce a new bargaining element in the negotiations, allowing for greater flexibility in the way workers are compensated. *Second*, severance payments could be unified and reduced for all permanent contracts and brought in line with rules in those OECD countries with a high employment ratio. *Third*, firing costs could be reduced by modifying the determination of what are "justified" or "unjustified" dismissals, since justified dismissals carry lower severance payments. Although economic reasons can be used as a valid argument to lay off workers with reduced firing costs, currently almost all dismissals are considered as unjustified when they are challenged in tribunals. Moreover, during the period in which dismissals are examined by the courts, the firm has to pay the wage (introducing a delay of about two months), which implies, in practice, many dismissals are unjustified in order to avoid delays.[50] Valid economic reasons for dismissals should be better defined.

Part-time employment has been made more flexible

An important element of the recent labour market reform is the change in the regulation of part-time contracts. Wider possibilities to work part-time are key for fostering female participation in the labour market. Part-time work may also play an important role in the development of some sectors (like retail distribution and tourism) which represent a sizeable share of value-added. A previous reform to encourage part-time employment allowed for a more rapid accumulation of pension rights (closing the gap with respect to full-time work), while social security contributions were subsidised temporarily if the new part-time job was permanent. However, the contract was not flexible enough in some respects, since part-time work was defined as 77 per cent of the normal working time (before 1998 up to 99 per cent), while the distribution of working hours during the year was too rigid. The new regulation returns to a more flexible contract, by eliminating the limit of 77 per cent and allowing for the concentration of "complementary" hours in specific periods of the year. These new elements are positive, as they help to adapt labour supply to fluctuations in production, and in conjunction with the maintenance of lower social security contributions should contribute to raising the part-time share to levels closer to the OECD average.

Wage bargaining should be decentralised

The wage bargaining system is in need of a deep reform. This was already recognised by the social partners in the 1997 pact, when they agreed to reform the present system (albeit with no tangible results). However, changes to the regulations governing wage agreements have not been included in the labour market measures adopted by the government in March 2001, although it intends to reform them quickly. Wage negotiations in Spain are complex and lead to an inflationary bias, as they take place at multiple sectoral and territorial levels, but with different systems across sectors. In some of them, like construction or banking, a national agreement is reached and applied in the whole country, while in most sectors national agreements (or recommendations on wage settlements by national unions) are re-negotiated at the provincial level, and then again at the enterprise level (for large firms). Opt-out clauses were introduced in the 1994 reform and allow firms to modify wage increases agreed in sectoral wage settlements. They are barely used, however, since they are subject to restrictive conditions (determined in collective agreements) and because firms prefer not to use them as an opt-out could signal weak performance to competitors. Overall, the situation is one where, on the one hand, national agreements which could help to contain excessive wage developments at the aggregate level do not apply and, on the other, wages are not negotiated at the enterprise level which could help to adapt wages to productivity developments at the firm level. Hence what may be the worst system – intermediate negotiations at the sectoral and regional level – prevails (Calmfors and Driffil, 1988).[51]

Reform has to be bold, because the multi-layer system of wage agreements is shaped by the vested interests of those who participate in negotiations at the local level. One reform option would be to suppress the intermediate level of bargaining and establish a national agreement for each sector, with negotiations (including an opt-out clause) at the firm level. Another possibility would be to require the explicit adoption of an agreement at the firm level, so that settlements would not apply automatically anymore. This would substitute the opt-out clauses by an "opt-in" system. The need for reform has not been apparent in recent years as wage moderation was prevalent while economic growth was strong. However, unit labour costs have started to rise above the euro area average, as bargaining takes headline inflation as a reference, which is higher than in the euro area. This, together with the increased use of catch-up clauses which applied to over 70 per cent of workers covered by collective agreements in 2001 and the feeble productivity development, could damage competitiveness soon and result in employment losses.

Active and passive labour market policies need to be carefully designed

In 1999, Spain spent 1.4 per cent of GDP on unemployment compensation, which, relative to the large number of unemployed, is low in international comparison. Net replacement rates in the first months of unemployment are high (OECD, 1999). On the other hand, eligibility conditions for unemployment benefits seem restrictive as compared to other OECD countries (OECD, 2000e). A single refusal to accept an adequate job offer or participation in a labour market programme leads to the loss of benefits. At the end of 2000 only 54 per cent of the registered unemployed received any unemployment compensation at all, due to long spells of unemployment. Although unemployment benefits do not seem to create large disincentives to job search, there are ways in which the unemployment benefit system could be improved. In particular, severance payments (which in some cases can be very large) should be taken into account in determining unemployment benefits. Moreover, benefit rights, which increase with time worked, are not lost after a short unemployment spell, which encourages firms to lay off workers for short periods (like holidays, for example) followed by re-hiring,[52] to avoid wage payments for that period with only a small loss for their employees. This provides an incentive to abuse the unemployment insurance system and should be changed.

Active labour market policies (ALMP) are managed to a large extent by regional governments (the exceptions being subsidies for permanent contracts and training for employed workers), although legislation is central and the general policy conduct is controlled by the State. The total cost of these measures, including employment subsidies but excluding the cost of lower social security contributions for new permanent contacts, was 0.8 per cent of GDP in 1999, which is lower than in most EU countries but higher than in the United States or Japan. Of this amount, training for the unemployed absorbed 0.12 per cent of GDP, and training for employees 0.10 per cent. International experience shows that training programmes reduce unemployment if they are narrowly targeted (OECD, 1994). In Spain, annual studies on the effectiveness of training measures for the unemployed are carried out by the public employment service (INEM), and they show a slight increase in the exit probability from unemployment for those who participate in training courses. Independent supervision might assess the potential efficiency gains in this area. Public employment services, which are in charge of the job search and counselling process, receive a relatively small amount of public funds (equivalent to 0.06 per cent of GDP in 1999), less than in many OECD countries with lower unemployment rates. They intermediate in only 17 per cent of new contracts, suggesting ample room for improvement. The recent decentralisation of public employment services has raised concerns about the lack of co-ordination across the regions, which is of particular importance given the large regional differences of unemployment rates (which range from less than 6 to close to 30 per cent). Although the roots of regional imbalances lie elsewhere, local services must ensure that information on job vacancies flows easily across the Autonomous Communities.

Spain has the highest rate of work accidents in the European Union. Work accidents have been on the rise, from an average of 6 483 per 100 000 workers in the period 1994-96 to 7 073 in 2000.[53] Apart from substantial human suffering, work accidents have a significant economic cost in hours lost. The Spanish legislation does not link social security contributions to the record of work accidents in individual firms, as is the case in many other countries. By internalising part of the economic costs of accidents, they would raise investment in security measures and move security surveillance from outside to inside the firm.

Product market reforms

The competition policy authorities need more resources

The main competition body is the independent *Tribunal de Defensa de la Competencia* (Tribunal), which is complemented by the *Servicio de Defensa de la Competencia* (Servicio). The Servicio, which is part of the Ministry of Economy, is responsible for the initiation, investigation and preparation of reports to the Tribunal, while the Tribunal is responsible for resolving matters but may also ask the Servicio to initiate proceedings. Sectoral regulators also exist for telecommunications (*Comisión Nacional de Telecomunicaciones*, CMT), energy (*Comisión Nacional de la Energía*), stock markets (*Comisión Nacional del Mercado de Valores*) and banks (Bank of Spain), although many regulatory powers are still in the government's hands. The Tribunal has taken a prominent role in the debate over regulatory reform in the 90s and has often been tough on practices that could restrict competition,[54] although it has only an advisory role on mergers, which are approved by the government. The Tribunal also imposes sanctions, and although these are similar to those of other European countries, they are low with respect to the size of the company and should be raised. A major problem for the competition authorities is the lack of resources: although human resources have increased they are still low, while the workload has grown considerably in the second half of the 90s.[55] The government may consider consolidating decision processes. A strengthened competition authority would also be better placed to fulfil its advocacy role in promoting competition. As a complement to national bodies, some regional governments are considering the introduction of regional competition tribunals to deal with cases within their territory.[56] Although this would allow a reduction in the Tribunal's workload, the setting up of new institutions could raise the overall cost of competition policy. Moreover, different criteria in assessing competition issues across regions should be avoided.

The Spanish authorities are committed to preventing high levels of concentration in key sectors of the economy. In some cases, concentration is due to earlier merger activity or to the sale of former State monopolies that were not broken up prior to privatisation. In others, concentration derives from mergers among the largest banks that own controlling stakes in many industrial sectors and utilities. The government has recently strengthened competition regulations in order to prevent concentration from damaging competition. In particular, a 1999 decree made the notification of mergers above a certain threshold compulsory, while a 2000 decree restricted the voting rights of any person or corporate representative who owns more than 3 per cent of two firms considered as main operators in certain key sectors. Moreover, in the package of liberalisation measures approved in June 2000, a new regulation prohibits agreed mergers from becoming effective while they are analysed by the competition authorities (following a similar practice at the EU level). At the same time, the decision deadline on mergers has been shortened from seven to four months. More importantly, in sectors like electricity or oil distribution, investment limitations have been established that will inhibit the expansion of dominant groups. All these measures go in the right direction, since they provide a safeguard against damaging effects from increasing concentration and pay close attention to the indirect control of ownership stakes by financial institutions; but they do not deal with certain inherited structures, and the competition authorities should stay very vigilant to avoid the abuse of a dominant position. The energy sector, for instance, shows a very high level of concentration and the new measures are unlikely to change market power significantly. In these cases, the authorities should be ready to apply further measures should there be evidence of an abuse of market power.

Subsidies to industry and agriculture distort economic activity

According to the EU State aid survey (European Commission, 2000), subsidies are below the EU average but are still high in Spain (Figure 15). Despite a decrease of almost 25 per cent since 1995, they amounted to euro 4.15 billion in 1998 (over 0.7 per cent of GDP). A large share funds specific sectors, like shipbuilding and railways (although public aid to steel production almost disappeared during the 90s) and the overall aid to shipbuilding, transport and coal production was reduced to 0.2 per cent of GDP within the period 1996-98. Subsidies to coal extraction are the second highest in the European Union (after Germany), and represent a heavy charge for small electricity consumers, who finance them through an electricity fee. Spanish coal is emission-intensive, its energy content is poor, and extraction would be unprofitable without public aid. Almost half of coal subsidies, however, go to development measures that promote alternative activities in coal producing areas.[57] In general, public aid should not be delivered in an *ad hoc* manner, but rather be concentrated on horizontal goals. Horizontal aid represented only 15 per cent of total aid to industry and services in 1998, while 4.4 per cent went to R&D activities (the same as the EU-wide average). To close the technology gap with other OECD countries and to raise productivity more rapidly, part of the substantial aid to specific sectors should be redirected to R&D activities, a process that has already started. Measures taken by the government boost scientific and technology development, including the creation of a new Ministry (Ministry for Science and Technology) with specific tasks in this matter.

Agriculture represents nearly 4 per cent of overall GDP and around 7 per cent of employment. Despite the rapid growth of exports after the accession to the European Union in 1986, the sector has continued to shrink during the 90s, while 700 000 jobs were lost. Productivity varies considerably across products and areas, with, for instance, very efficient fruit and vegetable production, but less efficient production of cereals and milk products. Direct support to agriculture from the European Union budget (decided at the EU level) is very high, representing about 25 per cent of the sector's value-added (and almost 1 per cent of GDP). Consumers also pay indirectly in the form of high prices, which are underpinned by stiff EU-wide import barriers.[58] Additional subsidies amounting to more than 0.1 per cent of GDP are provided by the Spanish central government, mostly to horizontal projects including insurance subsidies, emergency aid and irrigation infrastructure.[59] In addition, the government largely finances the special social security regime (whose annual deficit equals 1 per cent of GDP) and agriculture benefits from reduced taxes on fuel. In autumn 2000, after protests about the oil price rises, reductions in the

Figure 15. **State aid in EU countries**[1]

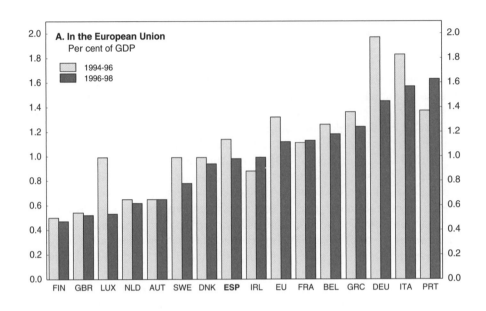

A. In the European Union
Per cent of GDP

1994-96
1996-98

FIN GBR LUX NLD AUT SWE DNK **ESP** IRL EU FRA BEL GRC DEU ITA PRT

B. As a per cent of total expenditure
1998

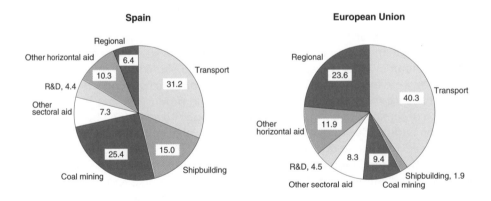

Spain

Regional
Other horizontal aid
6.4
10.3
R&D, 4.4
Other sectoral aid
7.3
25.4
15.0
Coal mining
Shipbuilding
Transport
31.2

European Union

Regional
23.6
40.3
Other horizontal aid
11.9
8.3 9.4
R&D, 4.5
Other sectoral aid
Coal mining
Shipbuilding, 1.9
Transport

1. Total State aid excluding agriculture, at 1997 prices.
Source: European Commission (2000), *Eighth Survey on State Aid in the European Union.*

income tax for farmers were agreed. Their budgetary impact has so far not been estimated officially.[60] Given the high level of EU-wide subsidies, national subsidies
should be lowered and focus on the restructuring of the sector. The high level of
subsidies distorts resource allocation and locks resources into low-productivity sectors, while encouraging production that would be unprofitable otherwise.

Water policy should focus on demand management

Despite the scarcity of water, Spain is among the largest consumers of water
in the OECD. Agriculture absorbs 79 per cent of total demand (a higher proportion
than in most countries partly due to the greater importance of this sector in the
national economy), but the price farmers pay does not even cover transportation
costs. Urban users represent 14.5 per cent of total demand, and their water is managed and priced by municipalities. After many years of studies, the government
approved a National Water Plan (*Plan Hidrológico Nacional*, PHN) in 2000, which
projects infrastructure investments of ESP 3 900 billion (close to 4 per cent of GDP
in 2000) over eight years, including a highly contentious water transfer from the Ebro
river in the north to the south-east coast and Cataluña (with a cost of
ESP 700 billion). The logic behind this project is that the coastal area has a very
dynamic agricultural sector, which produces a high proportion of agricultural exports.
Water in this area is scarce, with a high salt content and of bad quality. The area is
also heavily populated, with an important tourism sector that leads to a considerable water demand in the summer. The PHN calculates water needs by freezing
water consumption at the current level for areas where water is scarce (mainly the
east coast and some parts of Andalusia and Extremadura), while raising it in parallel
with projected growth where water supply is abundant. However, demand in the
past was boosted by the very low water prices and an appropriate pricing of water
could generate large savings. A market for water is currently difficult to establish
because the infrastructure is underdeveloped and historic water rights are not easy
to modify. However, water policies should use price signals as the main instrument
to restrict demand and promote an efficient use of water resources. Though the
available estimates suggest that the price elasticity is low in Spain, it has been
found in other countries that water demand becomes more responsive when the
price hits a certain level (OECD, 2000f). A new EU directive obliges countries to take
into account the recovering cost principle in pricing water by 2010 (transport and
management costs, an evaluation of the ecological impact and the scarcity value).
The Spanish authorities should implement this directive rapidly, as proper pricing
could heavily influence future infrastructure needs.

Telecommunication liberalisation is progressing rapidly

The liberalisation process in telecommunications has gained momentum
over the last two years, pushed by the activism of the sector regulator (*Comisión del*

Mercado de Telecomunicaciones, CMT) and by new legislation. Full liberalisation of the fixed telephony market was completed in January 2001, when the local loop was unbundled, largely meeting the deadline determined at the EU level.[61] Early in 2000 four licences for operating UMTS (third generation mobile telephone systems) were awarded through a beauty contest, and in 2002 the allocation of two more operators of mobile telephony with GSM (Global System for Mobile Communications) licences is envisaged.[62] Despite the progress made, some regulatory measures taken by the government to adapt to changes in technology or market conditions have been contested by some operators.

Prices of fixed telephony are capped by the government for the incumbent operator (Telefónica), and are still above the OECD average (Figure 16), although they have decreased substantially in recent years[63] and will be reduced further by 15 per cent between 2001 and 2003. The price structure of Telefónica, which was traditionally skewed towards low subscription fees and high variable charges, is being rebalanced. The re-balancing process will finish in 2003. As determined by the legal framework, Telefónica is obliged to publish its cost accounts before 31 July each year. This was an essential step to allow the tariff re-balancing of Telefónica and a cost-based determination of interconnection charges when the local loop was unbundled in early 2001. Access prices are determined for the moment at current costs, while long-run incremental costs should be implemented as soon as possible (as agreed at the EU level and recognised by Spanish regulations) as they are the most efficient pricing concept that allows competition on an equal footing by other operators[64] (and from virtual operators and resellers[65]), while they ensure that network investment is market-driven.

Access to the local loop is key for the transmission of data and Internet services. The use of the Internet in Spain is below the OECD average (Figure 17), although it has expanded rapidly in the last two years (more than doubled in the last twelve months). To promote the development of the information society, the government has introduced a new flat rate for access to the Internet to be applied to the dominant operator, Telefónica.[66] At the same time, the Reference Interconnection Offer (RIO) was adapted so that other providers could replicate the offers made by Telefónica. The new tariff has been contested by some operators as rendering services unprofitable. In any case, a new revision of the RIO is envisaged aiming to establish a more flexible approach for alternative operators and ensuring that interconnection prices reflect current costs. Other options to access the local loop are competing with traditional fixed telephony. One promising option for Internet and data transmission is ADSL (Asymmetric Digital Subscriber Line) and equivalent technologies,[67] which have been opened to competition via Telefónica's network, and have been adopted up to now by more than 85 000 customers, many of them small businesses.[68] Another option is the use of cable networks, which had been installed under a duopoly regime on a territorial basis (Telefónica and local operators) although it is now open to full competition.

Figure 16. **Telephone charges in selected countries**[1]
August 2000, in US$

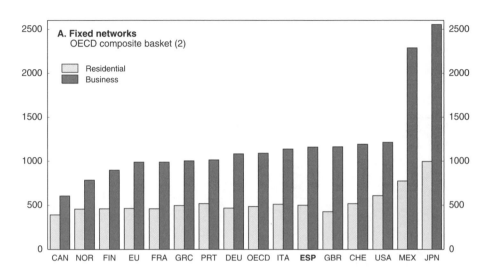

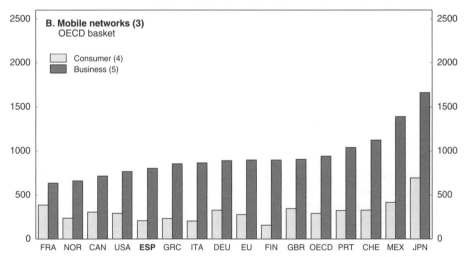

1. Fixed and usage charges.
2. Domestic and international services plus calls from fixed to mobile communication networks.
3. Selected companies. Charges including tax.
4. The basket includes 50 minutes per month and excludes international calls.
5. The basket includes 300 minutes of which 60 are international.
Source: OECD (2001), *Communications Outlook.*

Figure 17. **Internet subscribers in the OECD area**
Per 100 population, at 1 January 2000[1]

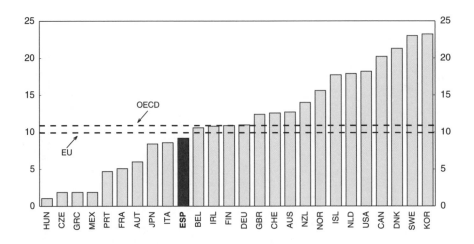

1. March 2000 for Japan.
Source: OECD (2001), *Communications Outlook.*

During the period in which Telefónica was ordered not to expand further in cable operations, investment was low because local operators had encountered problems in setting up networks on their own, but the number of users grew sharply. A further sharp rise is in doubt because Telefónica has reconsidered its expansion strategy in cable and is promoting ADSL technologies instead, which upgrade its copper line and also allow it to offer broadband services. Finally, radio access to the local loop has been set up in large towns with six companies offering services to business users.

As elsewhere, the market growth of mobile telephony has been impressive in the last two years, with the number of customers rising from 7 to 24 million, reaching a rate of penetration of 61 customers per 100 inhabitants. Three companies operate in the market with standard GSM technologies, and prices have decreased by 38 per cent since 1996. The CMT has indicated that the low number of market participants may lead to some degree of market power, and further measures to enhance competition are envisaged. The government, which shares its regulatory powers with the CMT, and retains most of the regulatory capacity for mobile telephony, has recently introduced number portability for mobile telephones and number pre-selection for international calls. To accelerate the implementation of new technologies, four licences to operate with UMTS technology[69] were awarded before the auctions of licences took place in the United Kingdom and Germany. After the success of these auctions in raising a large amount of revenue, and taking into account the high valuation of the spectrum revealed in these auctions, the budget law for the year 2001 increased the tax on the use of the radio-electric spectrum[70] from ESP 10 billion to ESP 150 billion in 2001 (0.15 per cent of GDP), though this could be modified for future years. In any case, companies will not be able to start operating on the agreed date (August 2001), since UMTS equipment will not be available at least until June 2002. Nevertheless, GPRS services (a standard between second and third generation mobile telephones) will be offered this year. In order to increase competition, the government has decided to issue two more GSM licences soon,[71] and to provide UMTS licences as soon as more spectrum is available.

These changes have been contested by affected operators. The current level of the tax on the radio spectrum, if applied during the whole concession period, is comparable in relative terms to the high revenues from auctions in other countries. The government is envisaging a reform of the tax, and should provide a stable formula that takes into account future market conditions. In general, the authorities should develop a framework conducive to investment. More competencies should be given to the CMT, who has been very active in promoting competition in fixed telephony, but has little power in the mobile market.

Electricity generation and distribution are highly concentrated

The Spanish government has made important efforts to open the electricity market to full competition, through a combination of privatisation and liberalisation. Liberalisation has benefited consumers, with electricity prices for households falling more than in the European Union. The 1997 reform law concerning the electricity sector outlined a liberalisation process that would have ended in 2007. The initial calendar has been brought forward to 2003, when provider choice will be extended to households. This is faster than required in the European directives. In June 2000 the government implemented restrictions on the expansion of the two largest electricity producers (Endesa and Iberdrola) to prevent further concentration in the sector (Annex II). Moreover, the conditions imposed by the competition Tribunal and the government during the merger negotiations between these two companies during 2000 – which under the merger plan would have reduced their production and distribution capacity but would have also increased their capacity to expand abroad – were considered too harsh by both companies and the merger did not go ahead.[72]

In the meantime, an open wholesale spot market for electricity has been established, in which generators sell power to large businesses. Bilateral agreements are also permitted, and a new market for future power will soon be implemented. High voltage distribution is owned by Red Eléctrica Española (REE), 40 per cent of which is controlled by the electricity generators, the maximum allowed by the current legislation.[73] However, the structure of the electricity market is not yet fully competitive. In generation, the two largest electricity producers control 80 per cent of the market. Because of the way the market is designed and its large share of production capacity, Endesa (the largest company) can determine the price in the wholesale market at least 54 per cent of the time (when demand is high), and Iberdrola (the second largest) 35 per cent of the time. Studies conducted by the sectoral regulator suggest that Endesa or Iberdrola, operating individually or collusively, could exercise market power, and that such behaviour could lead to an average price mark-up of 38 per cent above marginal costs. However, in June 2000 some important measures have been taken to contain the expansion of those two groups (Annex II). But competition would be enhanced further in the future if some of the new gas-fired power plants were built by newcomers.

The same companies that dominate in the generation market also control electricity distribution. Retail sales are open to any company, but given the degree of market power in electricity generation they are barely profitable without having generation capacity. Imports are very low, since total import capacity is small (around 3 per cent of the market). Existing contracts further reduce the available capacity of competitors.[74] Although some measures have been taken, further ones should be adopted to reduce the market power of incumbent operators. One option that has been implemented in other countries is to force companies to sell part of their generation and distribution assets, so as to allow for more market participants. This would require a change in the law. Several foreign companies are ready to invest in Spain (as shown by offers to buy the fourth largest company, Hidrocantábrico), and other domestic firms could show interest (for example, the smaller retail distribution companies). A second, complementary option would be to open up the wholesale market to imports which requires a connection between grids with neighbouring countries. If the environmental impact of a land connection to the European network is considered to be very high, other more expensive options (like a connection through the sea, which exists in several places in Europe) could still be economically sound in the medium term. A third option would be a clear separation of generation and distribution companies. European regulations oblige separate accounting of the two activities, but not separate control, which implies that regulatory surveillance has to be careful to avoid the dangers of vertical integration (like charging high prices to retailers and shifting profits from distribution to generation).

Other problems need to be tackled. Regulated tariffs (i.e. those for small companies and household consumers) include extraordinary payments for social and environmental goals that could be achieved more effectively by other means. As highlighted above, the domestic coal industry is still heavily subsidised, and this is paid by final consumers. Other add-ons to the electricity bill finance some of the co-generators and those generators using renewables in order to diversify generation sources. These subsidised prices are determined by the government, with no limit on the subsidy payments. Moreover, several regional governments charge for subsidies to renewables in their regions. Finally, stranded costs of the transition to competition are also financed by small consumers although the government established in February 2001 that these payments will depend on the price of electricity in the wholesale market, being reduced if prices are high. All these extra payments increase the price of electricity for households, which is one of the highest in the OECD (Figure 18) and should be reconsidered, although

Figure 18.   **Electricity prices in selected OECD countries**
In US$ per 100 kWh, 1999

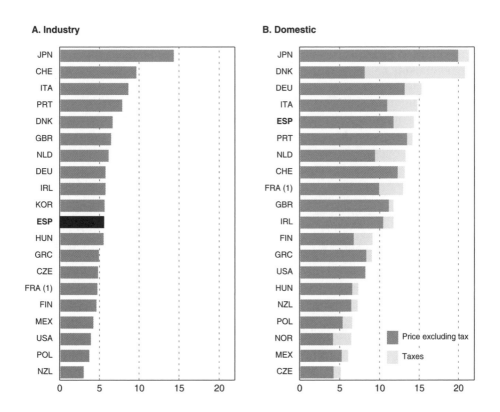

1. 1998.
Source: IEA (2001), *Energy Prices & Taxes, First Quarter 2001.*

household tariffs have decreased substantially since 1997: for the period 1998-2000, this reduction has been of 13.9 per cent, while for 2001 a further decrease of 4 per cent is planned.

Steps have been taken to enhance competition in oil distribution

Pre-tax oil prices in Spain are in line with the OECD average. Oil refining is controlled by three companies (Repsol, Cepsa and BP), to which the previous distribution monopoly was sold. Repsol, the largest producer, has a controlling stake in Gas Natural (the gas monopoly) while Cepsa is also developing a gas network. These three companies directly control a large share of gasoline and diesel retail sales, and also exert direct control through long-term supply contracts to independent retailers, who have complained about the dumping strategies of the large companies. In 2000, the government implemented a package of measures aimed at increasing competition in retail distribution. The maximum duration of contracts was reduced from 10 to 5 years (bringing them in line with recent EU regulations), expansion limits for the two largest companies in retail distribution were established, and the opening of new sales points next to hypermarkets, which were up to now blocked by local administrative regulations, was promoted (Annex II). Sales in hypermarkets could enhance price competition as has been the case in France and the United Kingdom. The market starts to show signs of increasing competition, price differentials have widened and independent operators account for a market share of around 20 per cent. In addition to measures introduced in retail distribution, measures have been taken in wholesale distribution and logistics. Transport and storage, carried out by a monopoly (Corporación Logística de Hidrocarburos) owned by the three major refiners, has been opened up to entrants, by limiting the stake of the three refiners to a combined 45 per cent (25 per cent for one company). To enhance transparency and fairness in the use of logistics facilities, new rules and increased surveillance of the regulator has also been implemented. In order to increase retail competition, the government should closely monitor measures adopted, especially the opening of new stations in hypermarkets, and should consider opening up the exclusivity contracts of petrol stations and obliging major refiners to sell part of the distribution business if anti-competitive practices are detected.

Liberalisation of gas distribution has been accelerated

Natural gas is an input of strategic importance, not only because it is cheaper and cleaner than other fuels, but also because it will be used as the energy source in all the new electricity plants currently under construction (equivalent to a power capacity of 30 GW [gigawatts], while existing capacity is 55 GW). Import and retail distribution of natural gas is still mostly controlled by one company, Gas Natural, which is partly owned by the largest oil refiner (Repsol), although some new importers and retailers have recently entered the market. The government has accelerated the liberalisation process in the sector. Earlier on, full liberalisation of the gas market was planned to be very slow, extending to 2015. The deadline was brought forward to 2008 in 1999, and further to 2003 in the decree of June 2000. At the same time, 25 per cent of the long-term supply contract of Gas Natural with *Sonatrach*, the Algerian provider of most of the natural gas consumed in Spain, will be auctioned among new participants in the market. By 2003 all consumers will be allowed to choose their supplier. Large consumers can already do so, while medium-sized ones will have free choice by the end of 2002. For distribution, new operators use the pipeline of E*nagás*, the only distributor, which is owned by Gas Natural and whose charges are fixed by the government. A new wholesale network access regulation is being prepared. As decided in June 2000, the capital of Enagás will soon be opened to other companies (Annex II) in order to ensure a fairer access to the transport pipeline, which is a key factor. Retail distribution is still a monopoly owned by Gas Natural (also at fixed prices determined by the government). The retail distribution network is still underdeveloped in Spain, and this has been used as an argument in the past to justify the monopoly power granted to Gas Natural. However, the ending of the moratorium on building new distribution networks for companies other than Gas Natural has been brought forward further from 2008 to 2005. This is welcome, but the ban on grid construction for other providers should be lifted more rapidly.

Despite recent progress, reforms are needed in the transport sector

The road haulage sector is liberalised, with prices set freely, and market access opened to every firm that fulfils the quality and safety requirements to obtain a licence. The sector is highly fragmented, with a large share of family businesses with relatively low efficiency. Although haulage does not receive any sectoral subsidies, tax advantages were given last year after demonstrations against oil price increases. Taxes on diesel are lower than those on petrol, and the size of the tax distortion between the two fuels should be reduced further. Passenger road transport operates in a regime of monopoly concessions for more than 3 000 lines, with prices fixed by the government. In 1999, the State privatised E*natcar*, the largest operator, and no longer participates in the market. Concession periods are long, although they have been reduced in 2000 from 8-20 years to 6-15 years to increase competition. The European Commission has proposed a new regulation that provides that contracts should be lowered further to 5 years when a government grants exclusive rights or financial compensation for public transport services, which may entice compensation payments to companies. Shorter concession periods, together with auctions of licences and the introduction of more than one line wherever there is enough demand, would increase competition while still allowing the imposition of universal service obligations.

As in most European countries, the railways are still a State monopoly (RENFE and a small company, FEVE), although liberalisation plans have abounded recently. Investment plans have been accelerated since 1999 after a period of low investment and loss of quality. Infrastructure investment and maintenance has been separated from services and a new company (GIF) that manages the infrastructure has been created. It will be financed partly through public funds and through fees paid by future railway service providers. Current plans foresee partial liberalisation in 2002 with competition starting in the long distance passenger service segment, the most profitable lines and the ones which have grown most in recent years. Lines will be assigned through a concession regime, similar to that for bus services. However, key aspects of the liberalisation process are still to be determined, such as the number of companies per line and the role of the regulatory body. The government should ensure that transparency is achieved in the concession of lines, if possible by auction, and that subsidies for universal service obligations are clearly circumscribed.

In air transport, the push for liberalisation (which started in 1994) has resulted in lower prices and better services. This year the government sold its remaining stake in Iberia (56 per cent), the largest operator, although plans to privatise airports have been postponed indefinitely. There are only three main participants in the domestic airline market, and some cases of collusion have been identified by the Competition Tribunal. In 2000, Iberia and the second-largest company (Air Europa) negotiated a merger, which would have created a near monopoly for internal flights if it had succeeded. However, the merger negotiations failed. Although much of the competition surveillance of airline transport is carried out at the EU level, the Spanish authorities should also remain alert, so that anti-competitive practices do not arise in the domestic market.

Other sectors

Land prices in Spain are high, partly because land sales and taxes are a major source of revenues for local governments. They have the power to issue urbanisation permits and are therefore able to limit land supply and sell their own land at higher prices. The central government has already attempted to relax the legislation on licensing, but the new regulation was blocked by the Constitutional Court since it curtailed the powers of local governments. In 2000 the government again attempted to reduce restrictions on land development by obliging local governments to justify any negative response to urbanisation permits, although the effects of this measure are still to be seen. Restrictions on land are not only detrimental to residential users, who pay higher prices, but also for the promotion of competition in some sectors (like petrol stations or retail distribution), and undermine entrepreneurship and economic activity in general. Although it is widely recognised that a reform of the financing system of the municipalities is a pre-condition for the liberalisation of the land market (OECD, 2000d), this has been postponed until a new agreement on regional financing is reached. The government should accelerate these reforms, and consider a simultaneous redesign of the financing systems of both municipalities and Autonomous Communities. It should also consider promoting the market of rental housing, which at 15 per cent is one of the smallest in the OECD, by reducing generous fiscal incentives to home ownership in the personal income tax and liberalising the housing regulations concerning rental further.

As is the case for the land market, liberalisation efforts by the central government concerning retail distribution are likewise hampered by the governments of the Autonomous Communities and municipalities. The legislation on commercial hours establishes at least 90 opening hours per week (raised from 72 in June 2000) and 12 opening Sundays per year (raised from 8). Regional governments are allowed to establish their own limits, but they cannot be lower than the national limits. However, almost all regions have stuck to the national limits.[75] Furthermore, some regions (like Cataluña and the Basque Country) have blocked the establishment of new hypermarkets, which need a licence to open from the government of the Autonomous Community. The current licensing regime should be liberalised so as not to inhibit market entry. Pharmacies are also subject to strict entry barriers, with restrictions depending on the minimum distance between establishments and on ensuring a guaranteed minimum population per pharmacy, though since 1997 it is regional governments (rather than the pharmacists' associations) who are responsible for providing licences. The fact that licences are transferred at very high prices reveals that licenses induce a substantial rent, which should be reduced by progressively eliminating restrictions on the opening of new pharmacies.

Financial market reforms

The banking system is adapting to financial disintermediation

The Spanish banking system has traditionally been branch intensive, which has been reflected in both high operating costs and high intermediation margins. The situation has evolved considerably since the early 90s towards a structure that is closer to that of other European countries and intermediation margins have declined significantly (Table 13 and Figure 19). This reduction has been compensated by higher income from non-interest revenue sources for commercial banks, and especially by lower operating expenses for both commercial and savings banks. Savings banks, which are specialised in retail banking and have a large pool of relatively unsophisticated customers, still have higher interest income than commercial banks but the difference has shrunk somewhat.

Table 13. **International comparison of bank profitability**

As a per cent of average balance sheet total

| | Spain | | | | All banks,[1] 1999 | | | | | | | |
| | Commercial banks | | Savings banks | | Spain | Belgium | France | Germany | Italy | Netherlands | Portugal | United Kingdom |
	1998	1999	1998	1999								
Interest income	5.5	4.4	5.8	4.7	4.5	7.2	5.0	5.2	4.5	6.5	5.6	5.2
Interest expenses	3.4	2.6	2.8	1.9	2.3	6.1	4.2	3.8	2.2	4.8	3.5	3.2
Net interest income	2.0	1.9	2.9	2.7	2.2	1.1	0.8	1.5	2.2	1.7	2.1	2.1
Non-interest income (net)	1.2	1.1	1.1	1.0	1.0	0.7	1.0	0.6	1.3	1.3	0.9	1.4
Gross income	3.2	2.9	4.1	3.8	3.3	1.8	1.8	2.1	3.6	3.0	3.0	3.4
Operating expenses	2.0	1.9	2.4	2.3	2.1	1.2	1.2	1.4	2.2	2.0	1.7	1.9
Net income	1.2	1.0	1.6	1.4	1.2	0.6	0.6	0.7	1.4	1.0	1.2	1.6
Provisions (net)	0.4	0.2	0.5	0.3	0.2	0.1	0.1	0.3	0.4	0.2	0.4	0.2
Profit before tax	0.8	0.8	1.2	1.1	1.0	0.5	0.5	0.4	1.0	0.8	0.8	1.4

1. Commercial banks for Portugal and the United Kingdom.
Source: OECD (2000), *Bank Profitability.*

Figure 19. **Bank intermediation margins and profitability**

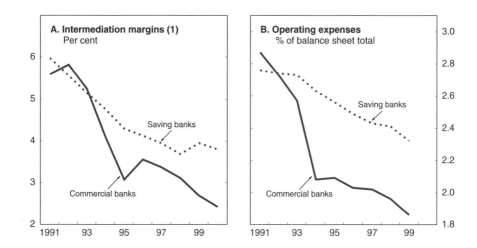

1. Difference between lending rates for 1 to 3 year maturities and deposit rates for 1 to 2 year maturities.
Source: Bank of Spain and OECD (2000), *Bank Profitability.*

Lower margins reflect financial market liberalisation, which has also led to financial disintermediation. The latter was influenced by the acceleration of the privatisation programme in the second half of the past decade that boosted the role of the stock market and helped to develop the financial culture of small investors. The sharp fall of interest rates in recent years also played a role in squeezing intermediation margins. These two trends and greater competition induced banks to participate directly in the disintermediation process (mutual fund management companies are mostly owned by credit institutions) and to introduce new technologies and rationalise and consolidate operations. Cost reductions have been reflected in the falling number of employees per branch, which has decreased from 9.4 to 7.6 for commercial banks, and from 5.6 to 5.4 for savings banks between 1990 and 1999 (La Caixa, 2000). However, the branch network is still dense, and has given a competitive edge to national banks *vis-à-vis* foreign institutions, which had relatively little success in entering the Spanish retail market when it was opened in the 80s.[76]

After the mergers of six of the largest banks into two,[77] the process of consolidation of commercial banks has come to a halt.[78] According to the Competition Tribunal, concentration has not become a problem for competition so far because there is still a number of medium-sized commercial banks and a large number of savings banks.[79] After mergers, the two largest banks have pursued a policy of consolidation in the domestic market and of expansion abroad. Personnel reductions have been achieved mainly through voluntary early retirement schemes, which are less costly than normal dismissals. As for non-personnel expenses, they are growing more moderately after a big boost to investment in technology in 1997. Geographic expansion into the European market has been weak so far, since it has led only to collaboration agreements and equity exchanges with foreign institutions.[80] In Latin America, however, the process of acquisitions that started in the mid-1990s (driven almost exclusively by BSCH – Banco Santander Central Hispano – and BBVA – Banco Bilbao Vizcaya Argentaria) has continued in 1999 and 2000. Currently Spanish banks control nearly 20 per cent of the Latin American banking sector.

Banking on prudence

Banking supervision is carried out by the Bank of Spain and is separated from that of other financial institutions (*Comisión Nacional del Mercado de Valores* [CNMV] for securities markets and the Ministry of Finance for insurance companies). Supervision is vigilant and Spanish credit institutions have to meet very prudent criteria in the calculation of their solvency ratios, which at present are comfortably above the 8 per cent required by the Basle agreement.[81] In 2000, the Bank of Spain published new loan loss regulations that oblige all deposit institutions to determine provisions based on default rates over the business cycle, rather than at a point in time. This will force banks to provide for bad loans during economic expansions by more than in the past, and thus avoids increased provisioning during recessions. While the new rule does not increase the overall level of provisions over a whole business cycle, it makes risk assessment more complex and requires a major effort of risk management by credit institutions. These will be able to establish their own risk management mechanisms to adapt to this rule, while a standard management framework has been approved for those banks that do not have the technical capability to develop their own models. This measure is welcome, since it provides a more efficient framework for risk management while at the same time it helps Spanish banks to adapt in advance to the new Bank for International Settlements (BIS) proposal to reform the Capital Accord.

The large market share in Latin America has raised concerns about the potential risks associated with macroeconomic fluctuations in the area.[82] However, Spanish banks have maintained management control of the banks they acquire. Moreover, risks are reduced because the Bank of Spain requires branches of Spanish banks in Latin America to conform to loan provision standards in Spain, which are usually higher than those in the host countries. The bank regulator has recently signed several agreements with its Latin American counterparts to allow for enhanced on-the-spot inspection of Spanish bank subsidiaries by officials from the Bank of Spain. Considering the higher risks in this area, a tight control of risks is warranted.

Savings banks' credit policies should not be distorted by political pressures

As in some other countries, savings banks in Spain concentrate their activities in the retail market, with higher intermediation margins than commercial banks, and a denser branch network. Since the early 90s, savings banks are allowed to open branches outside their regions, and have started to do so. A consolidation process is underway, encouraged by the Bank of Spain in the case of savings banks which are in a troubled situation and by regional governments, which has led to the merging of small savings banks into larger regional institutions. Between 1990 and 2000, the number of savings banks declined from 64 to 48. Despite consolidation, the number of branches is still increasing (contrary to the downsizing of commercial banks), as the networks of the largest savings banks have expanded to other regions. For the same reason, employment in the sector is also growing, and operating costs still remain considerably higher than those of commercial banks, although their profitability is also higher.

Savings banks do not have equity and are therefore not subject to surveillance by shareholders, although they are exposed to some market discipline because they will have to pay a premium on fixed-income securities if they underperform. While regulation is now identical to that of commercial banks, there is an asymmetry insofar as commercial banks can be bought by savings banks, but not vice versa. Recently some savings banks have considered issuing cuotas participativas, bonds that are quoted in the stock market and whose yield depends partly on the results of the savings bank. Although these bonds are supposed to introduce an element of market valuation, they do not give voting rights. Governing boards of savings banks are controlled by an array of institutions (mainly local and regional governments, personnel and founding institutions), and are subject to strong political pressures as their role is usually important in local and regional development policies. While this has apparently not affected the risk level of their portfolios, there is the potential for credit policy to substitute for or complement industrial policies by regional authorities. In order to avoid this, one option would be to privatise savings banks, letting market forces determine the channels of finance, and using more efficient and transparent instruments for implementing industrial policies. However, this is politically difficult as it is strongly opposed by the regional governments and technically complex. An alternative solution would be to limit the participation of political representatives on the board of savings banks, to enhance professional management and to continue closely supervising these institutions so that loan policies do not distort competition.

The banking sector needs to adapt to future challenges

Spanish banks have quickly adapted to the emergence of Internet banking, either through the creation of new subsidiaries specialised in on-line banking (like BBVA and BSCH), or through the development within the institution (like

medium-sized commercial banks and savings banks). There are signs that investment is slowing since Internet use is still low in Spain and the growth of this market is moderate. Over the medium term, however, traditional banking in Spain
could suffer from competition from Internet banking, possibly from foreign institutions. The dramatic reduction in transaction costs brought about by new technologies could damage those banks that, despite having developed an Internet
business, have to bear the costs of a high number of branches, still high operating
costs and difficulties in reducing the number of employees due to strict EPL. For
this reason, further rationalisation of operations to reduce costs, increase productivity and bring down spreads may become essential as competition increases.

Mutual funds intermediate a large share of investment

Several recent pieces of legislation and the 1998 reform of the Securities
Market Law have favoured the expansion of collective investment. The main elements of the reform were the reinforcement of supervision powers of the CNMV
over investment funds, stricter information requirements for funds *vis-à-vis* their
customers and the creation of new types of funds (funds of funds, master-feeder
funds and funds specialised in unlisted securities) that allow for more sophisti-
cated portfolio management. Placement restrictions were also softened by allowing mutual funds to buy unlisted securities and derivatives. These measures
should have a positive impact on mutual funds' performance over the medium
term. At the same time, taxation of capital gains in the personal income tax has
also evolved over the last years towards a more neutral structure that no longer
penalises investment in mutual funds. In 1996, taxation of investment income at
the household's marginal income tax rate (with lower rates for long-term investments) was substituted by a flat rate of 20 per cent for investment held for more
than two years. In June 2000 this rate was reduced to 18 per cent, and the waiting
period shortened to one year, which should boost competition among funds. The
reduction of the withholding tax on interest paid by bank deposits to 18 per cent
in 2000 has also improved tax neutrality, but together with the poor performance
of stock markets contributed to the stagnation of mutual funds in 2000 in terms of
managed assets, after a decade of strong expansion. The sector is now mature,
having reached a level of development similar to neighbouring countries, like Italy
or France (where expansion has also been very important in recent years), and is
now higher than in the United Kingdom, Germany or Japan.

Mutual fund management companies are mostly owned by credit institutions, which have used their branch networks to capture new customers. Fees are
still high, although they have been declining slowly in recent years. Maximum fees
are determined by the government, who reduced them in 2000 from 1.5 to 1 per
cent for money market funds, and from 2.5 to 2.25 per cent for other types of funds.
Following the new possibilities created by the 1998 reform of the stock markets, the

number of funds has expanded, while the portfolio of existing funds has been restructured significantly over the last two years towards a higher share of international assets. The use of the Internet is less developed than in banking, although it may grow more in the future as customers of investment funds are likely to be more demanding on prices and information because of substantially lower search costs. This factor, together with the increasing presence of foreign firms, should contribute to enhancing competition and lower fees in the medium term.

Stock markets must prepare for deepening integration in Europe

Since the Securities Market Law reform of 1998, new regulations have facilitated access to the stock markets. Administrative procedures to issue equity have been simplified and securitisation has been extended to assets other than mortgage loans. The regulation of takeover bids has been modified in order to put counter-bids on more equal footing with initial offers. Now counter-bids do not need to be paid in cash and can be compensated by other means. An important step in the promotion of corporate bond markets, which are underdeveloped in Spain,[83] is the new tax treatment of corporate bonds which is now the same as that of public debt. As a result, commercial paper issues in 1999 were six times larger than in 1998.

A new market (Nuevo Mercado) for "new economy" companies, regulated in a similar way to the Nouveau Marché in France or the Neuer Market in Germany, started in 2000. Companies quoted in this market do not need to show profits in the current year, but are only obliged to present their profit projections for the medium term in order to be listed. A special market for Latin American companies (Latibex) had already been created in 1999. The information and acceptance regulations applied are those of the home country, but the organisation of the market follows Spanish rules. Overall, the capitalisation of the Spanish stock markets has grown impressively in the last two years,[84] but it remains below that of major markets relative to GDP (Ortega Díaz, 1999). Trade is concentrated in a few sectors (banking, telecommunications and energy) and in very large companies. Spanish markets are clear candidates for future agreements with other European markets, and to this end the authorities should promote the harmonisation of domestic regulations with those of other countries. A first step in this direction has been the recent decision to "demutualise" the ownership of stock markets, that is, to separate membership and ownership of the markets, so that market participants are not obliged to own part of the capital of the stock exchange and participation in the capital does not necessarily imply participation in the market. In addition, a consolidation process is under way at the domestic level affecting trading, clearing and settlement systems.

Venture capital companies specialise in finding new business opportunities and developing innovative investment. Once the investment is mature, they sell assets on equity markets through initial public offerings (Leahy et al., 2001). The development of venture capital is important for long-term growth, and the low level of R&D

Figure 20. **Private venture capital investment**

Investment in early stages and expansion as a per cent of GDP, 1995-99[1]

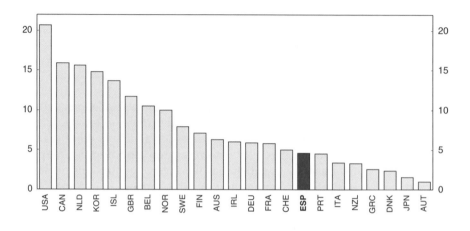

1. Data refer to 1995-98 for Australia, Korea, Japan and New Zealand.
Source: Baygan, G. and M. Freudenberg (2000), "The internationalisation of venture capital activity in OECD countries: Implications for measurement and policy", OECD, STI working paper No. 2000/7.

investment at the company level is considered an important factor for explaining the
low rate of productivity growth in Spain. Venture capital investment has been low in
international comparison (Figure 20). In January 1999 a new regulation on venture capital was approved that should boost this type of investment. A favourable tax regime
was granted to venture capital companies, by exempting 99 per cent of the capital
gains from the corporate income tax over at least two years. In June 2000 the holding
period to enjoy such an exemption was reduced from two years to one. Venture capital entities are supervised by the CNMV and must comply with established information requirements. A prudential regulation requires that they cannot invest more than
25 per cent of their assets in the same company, or more than 35 per cent in the same
company group. The effects of the reform are already significant. In 2000, 32 new venture capital entities were registered, bringing the total to 85.

Public sector issues

Decentralisation is advancing

The process of decentralisation of public expenditure has continued. By the
end of 2001 all Autonomous Communities will manage non-university education.
Health policies are already implemented at the regional level in 7 out of 17 regions,

and the negotiations for the transfer to the rest will start soon. This is in addition to social policies (excluding payments for pensions) and investment in regional infrastructure, which are already decentralised. Decentralisation of expenditure has gone hand in hand with personnel transfers to Autonomous Communities, although duplication is likely to exist as the total number of public servants has increased, despite the government policy (which applies to all levels of administration) to replace only one in four individuals that retire (Table 14). The deficit reduction realised during the second half of the 1990s was to a large extent based on restraint of personnel expenses, in particular wages. For the future, the margin of manoeuvre in these areas is limited, and hence efficiency gains will need to come from other policies. Among these, the negotiation of a new system of fiscal decentralisation between the government and Autonomous Communities, which is currently under way and should be implemented in 2002, should enhance fiscal responsibility by ensuring that spending responsibilities are more closely matched by revenue raising powers.

To replace the present system of fiscal decentralisation (1997-2001), the central government intends to establish a stable regime, replacing the five-year agreements that have been in place since the process of decentralisation started in

Table 14.   **Public employment and transfer recipients**

Thousands

	1995	1996	1997	1998	1999	2000
Total employment[1]	12 230	12 408	12 763	13 205	13 817	14 477
as a % of working age population	48	48	50	51	54	56
Public employment[2]	..	..	2 083	2 094	2 116	2 208
Central government	..	..	893	886	882	754
of which:						
Armed forces, police and justice	..	..	231	231	254	262
Public enterprises	..	..	61	60	58	58
Regional government	..	..	661	677	690	904
Local government	..	..	442	441	451	455
Universities	..	..	87	90	93	95
Persons receiving benefits	1 650	1 498	1 363	1 230	1 133	1 103
Social aid	191	155	123	100	82	69
Temporary agricultural workers receiving subsidies	216	192	193	202	211	222
Unemployment benefits	1 243	1 151	1 047	928	840	812
as a % of registered unemployment[3]	51	51	49	49	51	52
Government employment and benefit recipients	..	..	3 639	3 526	3 460	3 533
as a % of total employment	..	..	29	27	25	24

1. Labour Force Survey.
2. In July. Data from the register of public employment, not strictly compatible with Labour Force Survey data.
3. Including temporary agricultural workers receiving subsidies.
Source: Ministry of Public Administration, Ministry of Labour and Social Affairs, and OECD.

the early 80s. With the exception of the Basque Country and Navarra, which have special financing regimes,[85] the Autonomous Communities are financed by taxes which they can modify on their own (mostly on property and property transactions), by a 30 per cent share of the revenues from the personal income tax (PIT) collected in the region, for which they have limited leeway to modify the rates and deductions,[86] and by transfers from the State. Some of these transfers are earmarked, but most are unconditional, and are calculated as a share of the national tax receipts.[87] Since 1997 the central government has established a guarantee for the regions, ensuring that their revenues will be compensated if national tax revenues, or each region's PIT receipts, do not grow as much as nominal GDP at the national level. This guarantee has been applied in recent years, as receipts from income taxes have been feeble. Both guarantees are asymmetric, as regions are compensated if revenues are low, but do not pay back revenues when they are high.

The authorities intend to provide sufficient resources for the regions by better matching expenditure and revenue raising powers. However, the latter objective may not be easy to achieve. In principle, regions should be able to tax those bases that are not very mobile, in order to avoid displacement effects. Personal income is relatively immobile, but increasing the share of income tax transferred to the regions much beyond the current 30 per cent would risk concentrating revenues in a tax whose base is relative volatile. Consumption taxes (which are less volatile than PIT) would increase revenue stability, but their rates cannot be modified at the regional level as the tax base is fairly mobile. A regional variation in corporate income taxes could also create displacement effects. A good compromise would be to transfer a basket of taxes to increase revenue stability and to enhance fiscal co-responsibility through different mechanisms: First, revenue guarantees should be suppressed, and any re-distribution objective should be implemented through a separate and more transparent scheme. Second, the power to change PIT rates and credits could be marginally raised. Third, user charges for regional services, which are not fully developed could be increased (OECD, 2000d). Preliminary government proposals in the negotiations to modify the current system suggest that some of these elements would be adopted.[88]

Health care reform focuses on the control of pharmaceutical expenditure

Per capita expenditure on health care in Spain, allowing for differences in living standards across countries, is close to the OECD average (Figure 21). More than 75 per cent of all health care expenditure is financed by public funds, partly managed by the Autonomous Communities.[89] The authorities have succeeded in controlling expenditure since the early 90s, following the steep rise recorded in the previous decade. Total and public spending on health care have stabilised respectively at about 7 and 5½ per cent of GDP, which is below the OECD average (Table 15). However, this satisfactory aggregate performance in financial terms hides

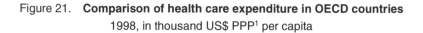

Figure 21. **Comparison of health care expenditure in OECD countries**
1998, in thousand US$ PPP¹ per capita

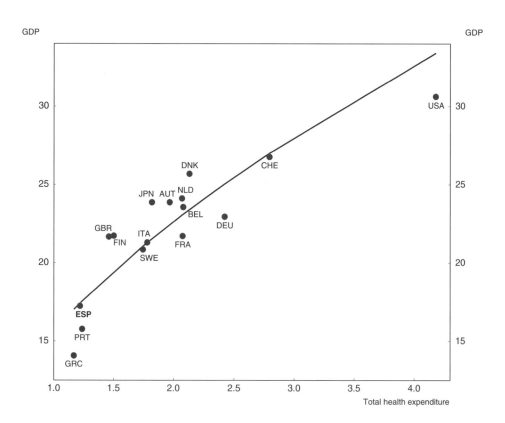

1. Purchasing power parities.
Source: OECD Health Data 2000.

some management difficulties. The number of hospital beds and nurses per inhabit-
ant is lower than elsewhere in the OECD. With only limited resources available for
hospital services, there is a persistent problem of waiting lists that are a cause of
real frustration and even incidents for the people who have had to wait too long for
attention. Moreover, pharmaceutical expenditures account for about 20 per cent of
total medical spending, a much higher proportion than the OECD average of about
15 per cent, reducing the resources available for other services, especially hospital
care. The annual rate of increase in pharmaceutical expenditure has remained very
high (over 10 per cent) since the early 1990s (Table 16). The authorities have therefore concentrated their efforts in recent years on controlling drug consumption.

Table 15. **Health care system indicators**

| | Expenditure as a % of GDP | | | | Expenditure on medicines, 1997 | | Per 1 000 population | | | | |
| | Total | | Public | | | | 1997 | | | 1998 | |
	1998	Change 1990-98	1998	Change 1990-98	% of total expenditure	User costs, as % of total cost	Hospital beds	Nurses	Doctors	Chemists	Dentists
Spain	7.0	0.4	5.4	0.2	19.6	7.4[1]	3.9	4.6	4.4	1.2	0.4
Austria	8.3	1.2	5.8	0.6	13.6	15.0	9.1	8.8	3.0	0.5	0.5
Belgium	8.8	1.4	7.9	1.3	8.1	18.2	7.2	..	3.4	1.4	..
Denmark	8.3	-0.1	6.8	-0.1	5.2	43.1	4.6	7.2	2.9	0.5	0.7
Finland	6.9	-1.0	5.2	-1.1	9.3	39.0	7.9	13.5	3.0	1.4	0.9
France	9.6	-0.5	7.3	-0.9	15.6	24.5	8.5	5.9	3.0	1.0	0.7
Germany	10.6	0.8	7.9	0.6	11.1	14.6	9.4	9.5	3.5	0.6	0.8
Greece	8.3	0.7	4.7	0.0	..	25.0	5.0	3.6	4.1	0.8	..
Italy	8.2	0.2	5.6	-0.7	10.4	11.1	5.9	5.3	5.9	..	0.6
Netherlands	8.5	0.1	6.0	0.2	9.5	1.5	11.2	..	..	0.2	0.5
Portugal	7.7	1.5	5.2	1.1	26.5	32.8	4.1	3.7	3.1	0.8	0.3
Sweden	8.0	2.1	6.7	1.9	10.9	23.9	4.0	10.2	3.1	0.7	0.9
United Kingdom	6.7	0.7	5.6	0.6	12.5	8.5	4.3	4.5	1.7	0.6	0.4
Japan	7.6	1.5	5.9	1.2	16.4	..	16.4	7.8	1.9	1.0	0.7
United States	12.8	1.0	5.7	1.1	3.3	..	3.9	8.2	2.7	0.7	0.6
Average	8.5	0.7	6.1	0.4	12.3	20.4	7.0	7.1	3.3	0.8	0.6

1. 1999.

Source: OECD *Health Data* 2000 and Farmaindustria, "La industria farmacéutica en cifras".

Table 16. **Evolution of pharmaceutical expenditure**
Percentage growth

	1980-90	1990-98
Public expenditure		
Total health expenditure	14.8	7.1
Excluding medicines	14.9	6.4
Medicines (a)	14.4	10.7[1]
Number of prescriptions		
Total (b)	..	1.4
For retired persons	..	3.2
For active persons	..	−1.8
Average cost (a) – (b)	..	9.3
	1986	1999
Memorandum item		
User charges (% of total pharmaceutical costs)	14.2	7.4

1. Based on data from the Ministry of Economy.
Source: OECD *Health Data* 2000.

The very moderate growth in the number of prescriptions suggests that most of the increase in pharmaceutical expenditure is due to steadily rising prices of medicines. Yet despite the rise in prices, which is reflected in a high average cost of prescriptions, and the existence of a co-payment system, pharmaceutical expenditures have continued to grow. One problem may be that the proportion of the co-payments, from which retired persons are exempt,[90] has been declining steadily over the last fifteen years. It has decreased by half since 1986, representing only 7.4 per cent of total pharmaceutical expenditure in 1999, one of the lowest proportions in the OECD. This would suggest fraud in the use of exemptions from co-payment. Pensioners accounted for 71 per cent of pharmaceutical expenditure in 1999, whereas this group represented only 16 per cent of the population.[91]

To slow the growth of drug consumption, the authorities have taken a number of measures to encourage restraint on the part of suppliers. First, mark-ups on refundable drugs were adjusted: in autumn 1999 they were reduced to 9.6 per cent of the sale price without taxes and they were reduced again by 6 per cent in June 2000.[92] For generic drugs, on the other hand, the pharmacist's mark-up was increased (from 27.9 per cent to 33 per cent) in order to stimulate this market. These products, which are on average 25 to 30 per cent less expensive than branded products, are not widely used in Spain. Their market share is only 2 per cent, compared with 20-25 per cent in Germany and the United States.[93] INSALUD (the central agency that manages health care expenditure in ten of the Autonomous Communities) has also introduced incentives for doctors to prescribe generic drugs.[94] Furthermore, since 1 December 2000 a system of reference prices has been in effect. It covers 590 medicines that are now refundable only as to the cost of the generic but not the branded product. The list of products will be reviewed each year and extended as the generics market grows. Finally, tighter budget controls have been introduced as regards public financing of pharmaceutical expenditure.[95] With these moves the government aims to economise ESP 63 billion and reduce the growth of pharmaceutical expenditure to 8 per cent a year. Annual growth of this expenditure item already slowed to 7½ per cent in 2000. These results are encouraging, but additional reforms will doubtless be necessary if the trend increase in pharmaceutical expenditure is to be curbed durably. First of all, it would be desirable to put an end to the overuse of exemptions from co-payment so that the latter may play an effective role.[96] To limit the rise in pharmaceutical prices, which seems partly due to a replacement of older products by new and more expensive ones without tested therapeutic value, the cost/benefit assessment of new medicines should be improved before they are made refundable. It would also be desirable to spread more widely the experience of Andalusia, where pharmaceutical expenditure has been better contained than in Spain on average.[97] In that region, district pharmacists monitor the prescription practices of doctors and inform them of pharmaceutical developments on the basis of comparative scientific studies. This provides a useful counterbalance to the publicity by laboratories. Another possibility would be to curb the pharmaceutical industry's promotional expenditure so as to reduce the incentives offered to doctors to prescribe new products. For the refundable medicines this promotional expenditure could be made subject to tax penalties as in France, or capped as in the United Kingdom. Finally, medicine packaging could be reviewed in order to reduce waste.

While it is important to achieve better control of pharmaceutical expenditure, the authorities should also continue their efforts to improve the efficiency of hospital management. A process of changing the legal status of some public hospitals to that of "public health foundations", with greater management autonomy, was begun in 1999. But at the end of 2000 the government announced the suspension of this process until the completion of the transfer of health service competence to all Communities, which should take until the end of the present legislature's term (2004). However, giving more management autonomy to hospitals remains necessary. A recent survey of 59 of the country's hospitals revealed that the best hospitals in terms of both care quality and efficiency were those under management practices closer to those of the private sector.[98] Efforts to rationalise health care expenditure should continue by, for instance, extending cost-benefit analysis of new measures and, in the case of hospitals, by developing indicators of care quality on a more regular and transparent basis. In this regard, the publication and standardisation of waiting lists and the introduction of contracts with users concerning the maximum admissible wait for different pathologies, as has been done in the case of heart surgery, would be a step forward.[99] At present the waiting lists are often not published and incomplete. Their management, which varies across Communities, is judged by the patients' associations to lack transparency, which poses an equity problem.

III. Ensuring the long-term financial viability of the pension system

In the coming decades, population ageing will affect Spain later but also more severely than in most other OECD countries. The strain on public finances will increase appreciably as from 2020-25. Given its low employment rate, Spain is initially in an unfavourable position as regards the ratio of older persons to the employed population. But the ratio of pension expenditure to GDP is currently lower than in most other countries, largely because of average pensions which are comparatively modest though growing rapidly. Moreover, the supply of social services available to the elderly is not yet very developed.

Thanks to the strong economic performance in recent years and demographic trends that are still favourable, the financial balance of the public pension system has improved since the mid-90s. It was at that time that the reforms, known as the Toledo Pact, were carried out. Negotiations between the government and the social partners concluded recently (at the end of March 2001) with the signature of a new agreement including an increase of minimum and survivors' pensions, an extension of the access to early retirement and the implementation of more flexible possibilities of transition to retirement. These changes, which seem compatible with the present state of the social security accounts, will not permit a response to the substantial challenge posed by the demographic outlook for ensuring the long-term sustainability of public finances. The distance in time and, in some respects, uncertainty about the threat tend to make reform efforts appear less urgent than they are in fact.

This chapter begins with a review of the demographic prospects for the next fifty years. It then provides an overview of the features of the system of assistance to the elderly, namely the pension, social welfare and medical care schemes. These institutional arrangements are considered from the standpoint of the generosity of benefits with respect to contributions and the incentives they offer for labour market participation. The implications of population ageing for public finances in the long term are then discussed. The chapter concludes with an analysis of the reform options that would meet the challenges posed by the demographic trends, which follow the general recommendations contained in the OECD study entitled *Maintaining Prosperity in an Ageing Society* (OECD, 1998).

The ageing process will occur later but will be more severe than in other countries

Over the past few decades the fertility rate in Spain has declined later but more steeply than in other OECD countries (Box 4), while life expectancy is longer than the OECD average (Figure 22). In these circumstances the ageing process will set in later but with greater intensity than in other countries (Figure 23). According to the latest demographic projections by Eurostat,[100] the total population will remain at its present level for the next 25 years and the rise in the old-age dependency ratio is expected to be less steep than the OECD average until 2025.[101] However, ageing should accelerate sharply thereafter. The total population will decrease by 10 per cent between 2025 and 2050, whilst the working age population will shrink by some 25 per cent. The old-age dependency ratio should rise much more rapidly than in the rest of the OECD area. Overall, it may rise by more than 38 percentage points between 2000 and 2050 from about 27 to 65.5 per cent, a steeper increase than in any other OECD country.

Spain has one of the lowest employment rates in the OECD area, which puts it initially in an unfavourable position as regards the ratio of older persons to the employed population. At the same time however, this situation provides ample scope to raise the participation rate and to lower unemployment to limit at least temporarily the impact of demographic trends. But an increase will depend on introducing substantial labour market reforms, raising the incentives to work to later ages and developing policy initiatives to better incorporate female and young workers in the labour market (Figure 24). The employment rate for men aged 55 to 64 is lower than the OECD average owing to frequent retirement before the statutory age of 65. In 1999 the average retirement age was 63.2 years for old-age pensioners and 50.3 years for invalidity pensioners under the social security general scheme.[102] If the employment rate does not rise, the number of employed persons per person aged over 65 is projected to fall from 2.2 to 0.9 between 2000 and 2050, compared with 2.9 to 1.4 for the OECD area as a whole. Average annual growth of potential output would decline by about 1 percentage point in the next 50 years as compared with the average growth between 1980 to 2000, and the growth of per capita GDP would be reduced by nearly 20 per cent between 2000 and 2050.[103] However, employment is currently rising and is expected to increase further.

Uncertainties surround these demographic projections but they should not be overestimated. The acceleration of the population ageing process as of 2020-25 is unavoidable. The different projections available for Spain point to much the same developments (Annex IV). They all incorporate the assumption of increased fertility. A steeper-than-projected rise in the number of children per woman would only have a limited effect on the old-age dependency ratio and growth of the working age population if, as will probably be the case, it occurs

Box 4. The fertility decline

The fertility rate has declined very steeply during the past few decades (Figure 22). Since the mid-1990s the average number of children per woman (1.2) has been the lowest – along with Italy and the Czech Republic – in the OECD area, whereas it was high (2.6) compared with other countries until the early 80s. The decline in the conjunctural indicator of fertility, which takes all female generations into account to establish an average fertility rate in a given year, has been particularly marked for the 20-29 age group, as young couples are having children later than before. The rate of completed fertility, which measures fertility per cohort, has also fallen but less steeply. For the generation born in 1960 it is now 1.7 in Spain compared with a European average of 1.8. If the completed fertility rate stays at its present level, the fertility rate should climb back progressively but to a lower level than in other countries, which is indeed assumed in the projections.

A number of factors have contributed to this decline. More and more young women are engaged in higher education, and this delays motherhood and tends to limit the total number of children they have. The fertility rate for women with a university education is 0.7, compared with 2.7 for those with less than five years of study. Spaniards are also marrying later than before as the result of longer studies and few children are born out of wedlock (11½ per cent) as compared with the European average (25 per cent). Surveys indicate that the present fertility rate is lower than the desired rate for economic reasons (lack of money, unemployment, need or desire to work outside the home, size of dwelling). For instance, child-bearing is postponed until one of the partners has found employment and the fertility rate of unemployed women is low, about 0.8. According to Ahn and Mira (1998), the very high unemployment rate among young males (reaching as much as 40 per cent for the 16-29 age group) and the insecurity of their jobs (70 per cent of these jobs are temporary) largely account for the steep decline in the fertility rate. This situation had a strong negative impact on marriages and births. An improvement in the employment rate and in the quality of jobs offered, especially for young male workers, thus appears necessary to boost fertility. Regaining confidence appears to be a slow process as the fertility rate started to pick up only in 1999, following several years of declining unemployment.

Little developed as yet, family policy in Spain has been unable to curb these demographic trends. Basically it consists of two tiers: direct welfare support and income tax relief. According to a study by Flaquer (2000), family support in Spain – which, unlike in other countries, is means-tested – is seven times lower than the EU average. Tax relief has increased following the recent income tax reform, but it has primarily benefited the better-off families. Very little is available in the way of home services and early childhood care (UGT, 1999), despite the growing need for this type of service with more women entering the labour market. Since female participation is bound to rise further, an increase in child care facilities would be desirable along with a development of part-time work, which is still underdeveloped (17 per cent of total employment) compared with other countries (30 per cent or more in France, Germany and Belgium).

Figure 22. **Fertility rates and life expectancy**

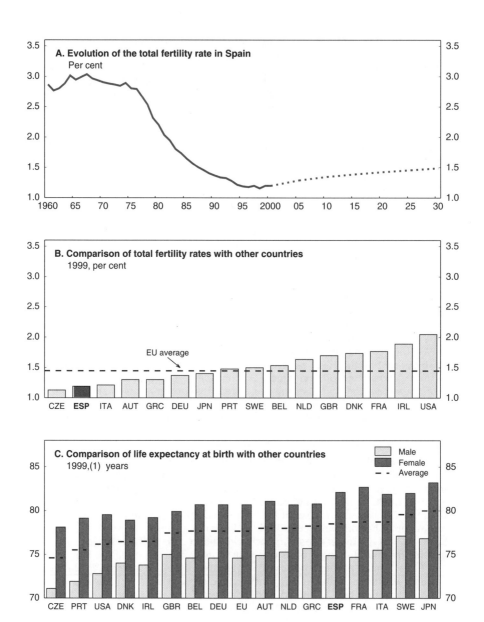

1. 1997 for Japan and the United States; 1998 for the Czech Republic.
Source: Eurostat.

e countries, they will be entitled to pen-
uld only have a temporary effect on the
ons assume a progressive increase in net
2010. Even higher net immigration aver-
a rate similar to the United Kingdom's
a decrease in the total population. The
then be about 7 percentage points lower
would still be higher (by 31 percentage
es.

the elderly

erly in Spain benefit from a pension sys-
s. The pension system has two tiers. The
vers the whole population. The second
ng rapidly. The public pension system,
cent of GDP in 1999, comprises a com-
rating on a pay-as-you-go basis (86½ per
tory scheme (4¼ per cent of public pen-
ot eligible for the contributory scheme
e types of pension (old age, permanent

mber of pensions and expenditure

nsion expenditure 1999		Number of pensions 2000[1]	
% of total	% of GDP	Thousands	% of total
100.0	9.6	8 755	100.0
86.4	8.3	7 607	86.9
58.4	5.6	4 141	47.3
13.2	1.3	1 577	18.0
7.0	0.7	859	9.8
7.7	0.7	1 030	11.8
4.2	0.4	654	7.4
2.8	0.3	457	5.2
0.3	0.0	77	0.9
1.1	0.1	120	1.4
9.3	0.9	494	5.6

upuestos generales del Estado 2001, and national authorities.

Figure 23.   **Population trends in Spain and old-age dependency ratios**
Per cent

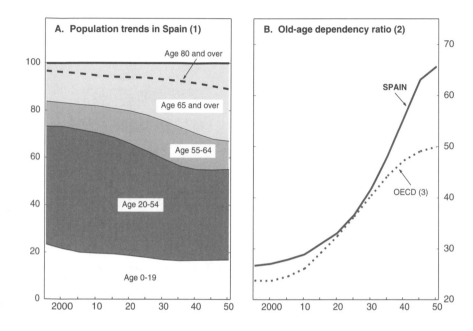

1. As a per cent of total population.
2. Persons aged 65 and above as a percentage of population aged 20-64.
3. Average of the rates of individual countries (excluding Mexico and Turkey).
Source: Eurostat, United Nations and OECD.

gradually (Annex IV).[104] Conversely, one cannot exclude a more moderate pick-up in the fertility rate than assumed in the projections. Moreover, life expectancy might lengthen more rapidly than in the Eurostat central scenario and accentuate the ageing process. The scenario assumes that life expectancy in Spain will increase a good deal more slowly in the coming decades than in other European countries, and than it has done in the past.[105]

The demographic projections are also influenced by the assumptions with regard to migration flows. Immigration has the advantage of producing an immediate and measurable effect on the working age population. There appears to be considerable

Figure 24. **Labour market situation**
By sex and age group, per cent, 1999

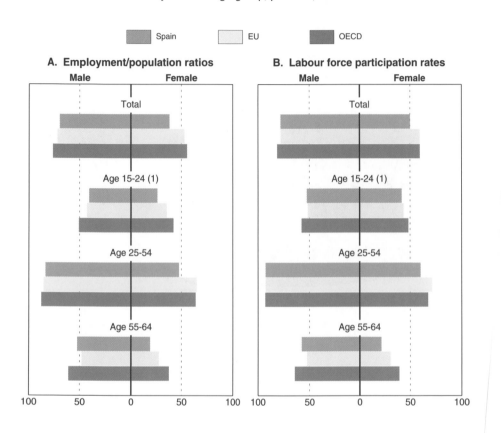

Spain   EU   OECD

A. Employment/population ratios

B. Labour force participation rates

1. Age group 16-24 for Spain.
Source: OECD (2000), *Employment Outlook.*

scope for increasing the immigrant population in Spain. Although Spain has been a net immigration country since the early 90s, the immigrant share of the total popula tion was one of the lowest in the OECD area in 1998 (Figure 25, Panel C).[106] Howeve increased immigration will not offset the effects of the ageing process, though it ma contribute to reduce them (Annex IV). It may also help to raise the overall fertility rat temporarily, although the behaviour of second generation immigrants in this domai often tends to be similar to that of the native population. It should also be borne mind that the political and social difficulties frequently associated with higher imm gration may limit the scope for this type of measure. Moreover, immigrants also ag

invalidity and survivors), are part of the social security system, which also includes health care expenditure, social services and family allowances. The contributory scheme covers all workers except members of the armed forces and the central civil service. Each worker is assigned to one of six schemes and the most important of them, the general scheme, covers most employees (including employees of local government and social security). Five special schemes cover farmers and farm workers, the self-employed, seamen, miners and domestic employees.[108] Members of the armed forces and the central civil service are covered by a special scheme (*Régimen de Clases Pasivas del Estado*) operated by the central government. Beneficiaries under this scheme account for less than 6 per cent of the total number of pensions but more than 9 per cent of total pension expenditure (Table 17).

Main features of the public pension system

The social security system has undergone numerous changes since it was created a century ago. The latest changes date from March 2001 (Box 5). They follow the 1997 reform, which implemented the recommendations of the Toledo Pact concluded in 1995 (Annex V). However, the measures adopted in both reforms have had only a limited effect on the rules governing the pension system. These remain more generous than in most other countries.

Box 5. The recent reform of the public pension system

The Toledo Pact signed in 1995 (Annex V), which led to the implementation of a number of reform measures in 1997, provided for a regular review (every five years) of the system. Within this framework, the negotiations between the social partners and the government concluded at the end of March 2001 with the signature of a four-year agreement. Various measures were adopted. They affect the following areas:

Entitlement to early retirement

– The possibility of taking early retirement in the general scheme was expanded. This possibility, which previously had been reserved for employees who had started to contribute before 1 January 1967, was extended to all workers provided that they have contributed for at least 30 years and have been unemployed for at least 6 months for reasons outside their control.

– For this group, early retirement can be taken as from age 61. The reduction in the pension benefit was lowered from 7 to 6 per cent for each year of pre-retirement for those having contributed for more than 40 years. The penalty is inversely related to the number of years of contribution. It is maintained at 8 per cent for persons who have contributed for 30 years.

Box 5.   The recent reform of the public pension system (*cont.*)

Possibilities for flexible retirement

– Under certain conditions still to be determined, workers over 65 will be able to combine a partial pension with earned income. Those still working after 65 will be totally exempted from contributions. A study will analyse the possibility of increasing to over 100 per cent the replacement rate for workers over 65 who have contributed more than 35 years.

Minimum and survivor's pensions

– Minimum pensions for under 65 year-olds were increased to the level of those for over 65 year-olds. The replacement rate of widow's pensions was increased from 45 to 52 per cent, rising to 70 per cent for widows or widowers with dependants and for whom the pension is the main source of the household's income. The age limit for entitlement to an orphan's pension was raised by one year.

Financing of the pension system

– As indicated in the 2000-04 Stability Programme, the allocation to the social security reserve fund will be raised to a minimum of ESP 800 billion (0.8 per cent of GDP) and to a maximum of ESP 1 000 billion (about 1 per cent of GDP) by 2004. The government will determine within one year the management rules of this fund (in particular the investment rules, and the rules of performance control and use of these resources).

– A deadline of 12 years was set for completing the separation of the social security's funding sources, with insurance benefits to be financed by contributions and social assistance benefits financed out of tax. In 2000, social assistance transfers still financed by contributions represented 0.7 per cent of GDP.

Virtually all the measures adopted should cause the pension system's spending to rise or its revenues to fall even if it will be partly offset by transfers within the government accounts. While no official estimates of the overall cost of these measures is available, it is clear that they will not improve the long-term financial viability of the system. It had been earlier planned to make the method of calculating pensions less generous. However, this has been put off to 2003, a year before the next parliamentary elections.

A system with generous parameters but paying low pensions

Retirement pensions under the contributory system are, as a general rule, awarded to workers aged 65 having contributed for at least 15 years. However, following the modifications introduced in March 2001, persons having contributed at least 30 years and being unemployed for at least 6 months can claim early retirement at 61. Pensions are computed on the basis of a reference income and a replacement rate whose level depends on the number of contribution years and age at retirement.[109] Persons retiring at 65 and having contributed for 35 years receive a full pension with a replacement rate of 100 per cent. Pensions are capped at the equivalent of 1.5 times the average gross wage.[110] They are indexed to inflation and subject to tax like other earned income. However, they are exempt from unemployment insurance and social security contributions; in the general scheme employees and employers pay 35.85 per cent.[111]

The retirement pension system comprises two distinct types of minimum pensions: contributory and non-contributory. The contributory scheme guarantees a minimum benefit for workers with at least 15 contribution years but whose entitlements are limited because of their low contributions. In the case the calculated pension benefit is lower than the minimum pension, there is a supplement called *complementos a mínimos* to reach the minimum pension level. The award of this supplement is means-tested and gave the beneficiaries a pension equivalent of about 30 per cent of the average gross wage in 2000. The non-contributory scheme pays a flat-rate benefit to low-income persons over 65 or disabled who are not eligible for a contributory pension.[112] In 2000 its annual amount for a single person was equivalent to 20 per cent of the average wage. The gap between these two types of benefit is being maintained in order to encourage people to contribute.

The parameters underlying the calculation of old-age pensions for private-sector employees are more generous in Spain than in other OECD countries (Table 18). In the majority of countries, pensions are computed on the basis of earnings over an entire working life and not just the latter part of it. The replacement rate is seldom more than 75 per cent, whilst the number of contribution years giving entitlement to a full pension is generally between 35 and 40. In most countries the average annual rate of entitlement accrual ranges from 0.5 to 2 per cent, much lower than Spain's 2.9 per cent. Yet despite this generosity, public pension expenditure as a percentage of GDP is lower than the European average (Figure 26). Thus the widespread opinion in Spanish society that "pensions are low" would appear to be confirmed by cross-country comparisons. Average pensions (all categories combined and without adjustment for the different tax treatment across countries) represented only 64 per cent of per capita GDP in 1998, compared with a European average of 75 per cent.

The situation of pensioners differs with respect to the generosity of the benefits they receive. A large proportion of retirees, over one-third, receive only a minimum pension.[113] Nearly one-half of the pensions of farm workers, self-employed persons and domestic employees, as well as survivors' pensions, are covered by the supplement to the minimum payment, as opposed to one-quarter

Table 18. **Main parameters of public pension schemes in selected countries**

For employees in the private sector, from 2000 onwards[1]

	Statutory retirement age (men/women)	Contribution period for full pension (years)	Reference period for benefits	Maximum replacement ratio (%)	Average benefit accrual factor[2]	Indexation of benefits	Minimum pension as percentage of average wages
Spain[3]	65	35	Last 15 years	100	2.9	Prices	20-30%
Belgium	65/61	45/41	Career	60	1.3/1.5	Prices	..
Finland	65	38	Career after 23 years of age	60	1.5[4]	0.2 to wages and 0.8 to prices	20-24% gross 30-32% net
France	60	40	25 years	80	2.0	Prices (basic scheme) Wages (earning-related portion)	..
Germany	65	45	Career	70	1.6	Net wages	..
Italy[5]	65/62	35	20 years	77	1.9	Prices	..
Italy[6]	57-65[7]	40	Career	No maximum	1.9	Prices	20-25%
Japan	60/55	40	Career	30	0.8	Net wages	..
Norway	67	40	Best 10 years	67	1.7	Wages	30%
Portugal[8]	65	40	Best 10 years	80	2.0	Prices	..
Sweden	65	30	Best 15 years	60	2.0	Prices	..
Sweden[9]	61-70	..	Career	No maximum	..	Wages and prices	..
United Kingdom	65/60	49	Career	20	0.4	Prices	..
United States	65	35	Best 35 years	41	1.2	Prices	..

1. Systems in place or reforms already adopted.
2. Maximum replacement ratio divided by the contribution period for a full pension.
3. As from 2002.
4. 2.5 from 60 years of age onwards.
5. For years in employment before 1996.
6. New system (Dini reform).
7. The statutory age of retirement is (for both men and women) from 57 until 65. The coefficients of transformation actuarially adjust for the different age of retirement.
8. A reform is under way.
9. New system. If wage growth is 1.6 per cent benefits will be adjusted to inflation, if lower than 1.6 per cent benefits will be adjusted less than inflation.
Source: OECD calculations and Chand, S.K. and A. Jaeger, "Aging Populations and Public Pensions Schemes", IMF Occasional Paper No. 147, December 1996.

Figure 26. **Pension expenditure in selected countries**

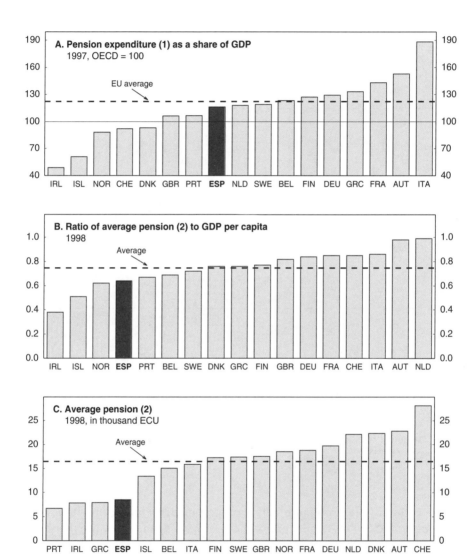

1. Pension expenditure shown here is the sum of public expenditure on old-age and disability cash benefits plus survivors pension. Differences in the tax treatment of pensions across countries are not taken into account. The OECD total excludes Hungary.
2. Cash payments for persons aged over 65 for disability, old-age and survivors.
Source: Eurostat, Sespros database, January 2000; OECD, Social Expenditure database, 2000 and OECD calculations.

Figure 27. **Pensions benefiting from the minimum complement**
As a per cent of total pensions, July 1999

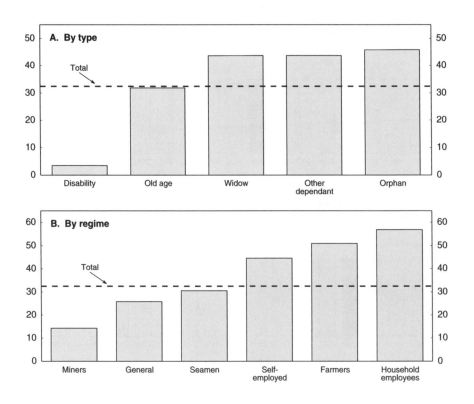

Source: Ministry of Labour and Social Affairs, *Informe Económico Financiero a los Presupuestos de la Seguridad Social, Año 2000.*

for the general scheme (Figure 27). Average pensions under the main special schemes amounted to 30 per cent of the average wage in 1999, the figure being 27 per cent for widows' pensions, as against 55 per cent for old-age pensions under the general scheme. The pensions of central government civil servants, on the other hand, are higher (Box 6). It is estimated that they are about one-third higher than the pensions of other employees. There are also major differences between the youngest and the oldest retirees. In 1999 old-age pensions for new retirees under the general scheme were 25 per cent higher than the average retirement pension, amounting to nearly 70 per cent of the average wage.

Box 6.   **The pension scheme for central government civil service employees**

The pension scheme for employees of central government (*Régimen de Clases Pasivas del Estado*) and the social security general scheme are similar in many respects but very different in others. The main differences between the two schemes, which concern the method of pension calculation and early retirement possibilities, are as follows:

Pension calculation

- Employees may opt for retirement between the ages of 65 and 70, when it becomes compulsory.

- Pensions are computed on a reference income and a replacement rate. The reference income is not directly related to earnings. It is determined by regulations and with little transparency as a fixed amount for each of five categories of civil servants. This reference income is generally lower than the employees' actual earnings.

- The replacement rate depends only on the number of contribution years. For those having contributed for 35 years, the replacement rate is 100 per cent. For those having reached the age of 65, the accrual of pension rights is slower than in the general scheme. At that age the replacement rate is 81.7 per cent after 30 contribution years, against 90 per cent in the general scheme.

Early retirement

- The system is very generous to employees taking early retirement as agents' age does not affect the replacement ratio, contrary to the general scheme. Those having contributed for at least 30 years can retire at 60 without any penalty. After 30 years of contribution the replacement rate is 81.7 per cent, compared with 54 per cent for the general scheme. Since 1984, the number of early retirees has amounted to about a third of the number of civil servants that entered the pension scheme.

It is estimated that pensions in this scheme are on average one-third higher than those paid by the general scheme. This difference is no doubt due in part to the population segment involved, which receives comparatively high pay. In addition, civil service careers are not interrupted by unemployment. The greater generosity towards early retirees than in the general scheme is probably another reason for the difference in average pension levels between the two schemes.

The manner in which the central government scheme is financed lacks transparency. Employee contributions, which are of the order of 6 to 7 per cent, differ according to government sector. They are supplemented by a (notional) contribution from the State as employer, the amount of which is not explicit as in the private sector, although it appears in the national accounts. This makes it difficult to gauge the financial difficulties that the scheme may encounter in the future.

The present low level of pensions is essentially attributable to four factors. *First*, careers had often been interrupted by unemployment spells and/or shortened by early retirement due to labour market difficulties.[114] In 1998 only 60 per cent of all retirement pensions had been taken after 35 contribution years and, in the case of the general scheme, less than 50 per cent of pensioners had reached the statutory retirement age of 65 (Table 19). This has had the effect of reducing the reference base and/or the earnings replacement rate on which pensions are computed. *Second*, the inflation-indexing system tends to lower the relative level of benefit for the oldest age groups. *Third*, women – because of their low labour market participation and long life expectancy – often have no more than the minimum widow's pension as their sole income source. They represented more than half of the benefits received by women, as opposed to less than 10 per cent in the case of men.[115] *Fourth*, the method used to finance the main special schemes generates incentives for workers to limit their contributing periods and receive a minimum pension. These two last factors are the main reason for the present low level of pensions.

In contrast with the general scheme, the contribution bases for farm workers and domestic employees are not earnings-related. They are statutory fixed amounts set at low levels. The self-employed may freely choose their contribution base within a fixed range, but the upper limit has been lowered to hold pension entitlements down. These restrictions reduce the pensions that self-employed persons may claim. As shown in Table 20 (Panel A), for equivalent earnings (corresponding to the mean wage) the estimated replacement rate for farm workers and

Table 19.   **Retirement age and contribution duration for earnings-related pension schemes**

Per cent

	General	Farmers	Self-employed	Household employees	Seamen	Miners	Total
Persons taking their retirement at age:[1]							
60 or less	26.6	3.8	4.8	3.1	67.6	57.2	17.8
61 to 64	27.6	2.1	6.0	3.0	14.5	21.5	17.4
65 or over	45.8	94.1	89.2	93.9	17.9	21.3	64.9
Average (in years)	62.5	64.8	64.6	64.8	61.3	61.7	63.2
Persons having contributed for:[2]							
15 years	1.1	12.3	11.6	19.8	1.2	0.0	5.0
16 to 25 years	11.6	20.7	39.4	61.3	8.5	1.4	18.4
26 to 34 years	15.9	14.7	26.6	12.3	31.3	5.7	17.3
35 years	71.4	52.3	22.5	6.7	59.1	92.9	59.2
Average (in years)	32.4	28.7	25.4	20.8	32.3	34.6	30.2

1. 1999.
2. 1998.
Source: Ministry of Labour and Social Affairs, *Informe Económico Financiero a los Presupuestos de la Seguridad Social, Año 2000*, and Bank of Spain, Directorate General, Research Department.

Table 20. **Replacement rates and rates of return for the main earnings-related pension schemes**

Relative to average earnings in 2000

	Units	General[1]	Farmers[2]	Self-employed[3]	Household employees
A. For a full career					
Retirement age	Years	65	65	65	65
Contribution period	Years	35	35	35	35
Replacement rate[4]	%	88.7	35.3	84.0	33.2
Internal rate of return	%	4.1	5.7	6.4	5.1
B. For an average career (end 1990s)					
Retirement age	Years	63	65	65	65
Contribution period	Years	32	29	25	21
Replacement rate[4]	%	70.1	31.0	67.4	30.3
Internal rate of return	%	4.0	6.5	7.7	8.9
C. For an extra year of contribution[5]					
Change compared to an average career:					
Replacement rate[4]	%	8.9	0.7	1.6	0.0
Internal rate of return	%	0.1	−0.2	−0.2	−0.5
Pension wealth	%	18.5	−2.7	−0.6	−7.0
Memorandum items					
For a full career					
Relative to 1½ times average earnings					
Replacement rate[4]	%	88.7	23.5	56.1	22.1
Internal rate of return	%	4.1	5.7	6.4	5.1

1. Assuming the worker belongs to category 2.
2. Self-employed farmers.
3. Assuming that contributions for the first years are made at the minimum rate.
4. On gross wages.
5. The retirement age would increase to age 64 for the general pension scheme but would remain at age 65 for the others.
Source: OECD.

domestic employees with a full career does not exceed 40 per cent, as compared with 89 per cent for employees in the general scheme. Furthermore, the combined effect of these restrictions on contributions and the existence of a minimum pension is to shorten the contribution period. In 1998, 33 per cent of farm workers, 51 per cent of self-employed persons and 81 per cent of domestic employees contributed for less than 25 years, compared with 13 per cent of employees in the general scheme (Table 19). When these workers' contribution period increases, their pension wealth decreases as does the implicit rate of return on their contributions, which reduces their incentive to contribute more (Table 20, Panel C).[116]

The system's internal rate of return is high, particularly in the special schemes

As in the funded systems, in a PAYG (pay-as-you-go) system, the degree of generosity can be estimated by the internal rate of return that equalises the discounted value of contributions paid with that of pensions received. As Samuelson (1958) has shown, the system's internal rate of return must be less than or equal to the real rate of output growth in order to keep the scheme in equilibrium (Annex VI). The OECD has made estimates of the rates of return for the different pension schemes, taking into account the average retirement age and length of contribution at the end of the 1990s. The results show real rates of return ranging from 6½ to 9 per cent for the pension schemes for farm workers, the self-employed and domestic employees, as against 4 per cent for the general scheme (Table 20, Panel B).[117] These rates of return are high in comparison with other OECD countries (Boldrin *et al.*, 1999).[118] They are also high relative to the long-term growth prospects of the economy, even taking into account an increase in the employment rate, whose effect will be only temporary in any case. Strong financial imbalances in the pension system should thus emerge in the future (see below). The large differences of returns between regimes indicate also the high degree of redistribution within the system. Although pensions in the main special schemes are low on the whole, they provide beneficiaries with a much higher return on contributions than the general scheme offers.[119] Within the general scheme, the internal rates of return and replacement rates vary according to the level and growth path of employees' real earnings and their life expectancy (Table 21). Owing to the existence of minimum and maximum pensions, the replacement rate is for instance higher for the lowest income bracket than for the upper bracket. But the internal rate of return for pensions falls only slightly when earnings increase, due to the existence of the contribution floor and ceiling.

The financial balance of the system has improved but some schemes are in structural disequilibrium

Pensions, which are indexed only to consumer prices, have risen on average much more rapidly than earnings over the past 20 years (Table 22). This trend, which is due mainly to the substitution of new and higher pensions for old and lower pensions, is likely to continue. Careers will lengthen as a result of falling unemployment. With more women in the labour market, the proportion of minimum pensions should fall and retirement pensions increase. The proportion of minimum pensions fell from 48 per cent of total pensions in 1983 to 33 per cent in 1999. Relative to new pensions awarded in 1999, the proportion was about one-fourth. In addition to the pension system's generous parameters, survivor's pensions can be cumulated with old-age pensions because they are not means-tested,[120] which is usually not the case in other countries and is liable to prove costly for the system in the future. Moreover, the index mechanism, although confined to price inflation and therefore not equitable for older pensioners, may also prove generous in certain circumstances, notably because of its asymmetric implementation. Pensions are pegged to projected inflation, with compensation if the forecasts are exceeded. But when inflation is less than projected, as

Table 21. **Replacement rates and rates of return for the general pension scheme**

For a full career with 35 years of contributions and retirement at age 65 in 2000, per cent

Depending on remuneration level						
Per cent of average gross wage[1]	**35.7**[2]	**50**	**75**	**100**	**150**	**300**
Annual growth of real remuneration	1.7	1.7	1.7	1.7	1.7	1.7
Life expectancy (years)	80	80	80	80	80	80
Replacement rate on gross wage	88.8	88.7	88.7	88.7	88.7	51.2
Replacement rate on net wage	94.9	94.7	94.7	94.7	94.2	53.2
Internal rate of return	4.1	4.1	4.1	4.1	4.0	4.0
Depending on productivity growth level						
Per cent of average gross wage[1]	100	100	100	100	100	100
Annual growth of real remuneration	**0.5**	**1.0**	**1.5**	**1.7**	**2.0**	**2.5**
Life expectancy (years)	80	80	80	80	80	80
Replacement rate on gross wage	96.2	93.0	89.9	88.7	87.0	84.2
Replacement rate on net wage	102.7	99.3	96.0	94.7	92.9	89.9
Internal rate of return	3.5	3.8	4.0	4.1	4.3	4.5
Depending on life expectancy level						
Per cent of average gross wage[1]	100	100	100	100	100	100
Annual growth of real remuneration	1.7	1.7	1.7	1.7	1.7	1.7
Life expectancy (years)	**77**	**78**	**79**	**80**	**81**	**82**
Replacement rate on gross wage	88.7	88.7	88.7	88.7	88.7	88.7
Replacement rate on net wage	94.7	94.7	94.7	94.7	94.7	94.7
Internal rate of return	3.5	3.7	3.9	4.1	4.3	4.4

1. The professional category 1 defining the minimum and maximum contribution basis has been used in the case of a remuneration representing 300 per cent of the average gross wage and the professional category 5-7 in the case of a remuneration representing 35.7 and 50 per cent of this wage. Category 2 has been used in the other cases.
2. This ratio corresponds to the minimum wage.
Source: OECD.

Table 22. **Expenditure of earnings-related pension schemes**

Annual growth, per cent

	1981-90	1990-95	1995-2000[1]	1981-2000[1]
Total expenditure	14.6	10.4	6.4	11.3
Number of pensions	3.3	2.6	1.7	2.7
Average pension	11.0	7.6	4.6	8.4
of which:				
Indexation and other revaluation effects[2]	8.1	5.2	2.7	5.9
Other effects	2.7	2.2	1.8	2.3
Real average pension (a)	2.0	1.9	1.9	1.9
Real compensation per employee (b)	0.2	1.5	0.4	0.6
Difference (a) − (b)	1.9	0.4	1.5	1.4
Memorandum items				
Number of contributors	2.5	-0.6	3.7	2.0
Productivity	2.3	2.4	0.4	1.8
Inflation (private consumption deflator)	8.8	5.6	2.7	6.3

1. Estimate.
2. Includes increases in minimum pensions.
Source: Ministry of Labour and Social Affairs, *Informe Económico Financiero a los Presupuestos de la Seguridad Social, Año 2000*; Bank of Spain, Directorate General, Research Department and OECD.

between 1996 and 1998, no adjustment is made, with the result that pensions increase in real value.[121] Full inflation-adjustment also means that, unlike real wages, pensions do not have to adjust in real terms to an adverse supply shock like the recent oil price rise.

Despite the continuing rise in average pensions, the system's financial balance has improved appreciably in recent years, although there are still major imbalances between the different contributory schemes. All told, the social security system showed a surplus of 0.5 per cent of GDP in 2000, compared with a deficit of 0.7 per cent in 1995.[122] However, only the general scheme and the scheme for self-employed persons posted surpluses in 2000. Their combined surplus, equivalent to about 1½ per cent of GDP, was almost entirely offset by the deficits of the other schemes, particularly the farm workers' scheme, where receipts cover less than 20 per cent of expenditure. The steep increase in the number of contributors, which is linked to strong growth and the labour market reform, is mainly responsible for the improvement in the overall financial situation. The rise in the average number of contributors per pension from 2.07 to 2.28 between 1995 and 2000 has also been affected by the retirement of the small age groups born during the civil war and reduced recourse to early retirement (see below). By contrast, the structural financial imbalance of certain special schemes can be explained in part by the small number of contributors per pension. But it is also due to the small size of the contribution bases and, in some cases, to the low contribution rates of these schemes and the short periods of contribution.[123] The farm workers' scheme accounted for 7.5 per cent of all pension contributors, but its contributions represented no more than 2.5 per cent of pension contributions as a whole.

The ongoing separation of social security finances should keep the public retirement schemes in surplus during the next years. The social security system, which covers the contributory and non-contributory PAYG schemes, is financed by social insurance contributions and transfers from the central government budget. The share of transfers from central government used to finance the non-contributive social benefits (including health care spending), which amounted to 5 per cent of GDP in 1999 against 10 per cent for contributions, has increased during the past few years. It should increase further with the continuing process of separating pension funding sources according to whether their purpose is assistance or insurance (Annex V).[124] The social security surpluses, which should also benefit from the fact that demographic pressures remain low for the time being, should make it possible to increase the endowment of the reserve fund set up in 1999 in accordance with the recommendations of the Toledo Pact. This is one of the targets of the latest Stability Programme, which aims to increase the fund's resources from 0.2 per cent of GDP at present, if the allocations set for 2001 are taken into account, to 1 per cent of GDP by 2004 (Chapter I).

Early retirement has declined in recent years

As in many other European countries, early retirement was long regarded as instrumental for coping with employment reductions related to corporate restructuring. With intensive use of various early retirement schemes, the actual age at retirement declined steeply in the 70s and 80s, as it did in many OECD countries, the result being a fall in the participation rate for men aged 55 to 64 (Figure 28).[125] Since the mid-90s, however, the trend has shifted. The participation rate for older workers has risen and the mean actual retirement age has stabilised at just over 63 years. A number of factors have contributed; among these, the change in the population's age structure and level of education seems to have played an important part. The rate of transition to retirement is lower for the most skilled and the latter's presence among older workers has increased since the beginning of the 90s and should continue to rise in the future.[126] Use of early retirement schemes has lessened as a result of the improved business climate since 1995 and because some of the schemes have progressively become less generous. The measures adopted in March 2001 have however extended the possibilities of taking early retirement to new groups of agents.

A number of arrangements, whose features vary, encourage retirement before the statutory age of 65. The most important arrangement is the one in the

Figure 28. **Participation rates for population aged 55-64**
Per cent

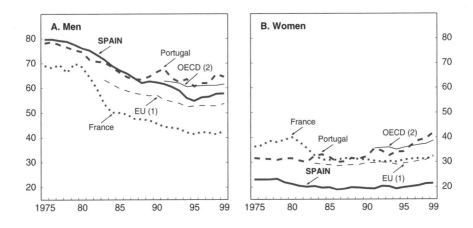

1. Excluding Austria up to 1993 inclusive.
2. Excluding Hungary; for 1991-93 also excluding Austria and the Czech Republic.
Source: OECD (2000), *Labour Force Statistics, Part III.*

general scheme allowing employees, since March 2001, to take retirement as from 61 if they have contributed for at least 30 years and have been unemployed for the last 6 months.[127] The pension is then reduced by a rate of 6 to 8 per cent per year of pre-retirement, depending on the number of contribution years, making a total reduction of 40 per cent for a worker that has contributed for 30 years. In 1999 nearly 55 per cent of new pensioners had retired early. The pension benefit calculation, which allows rapid accrual of pension rights early in a career[128] and guarantees a minimum benefit, encourages early retirement for certain categories of workers. Estimates by the OECD indicate that, for workers with low earnings (equivalent to the minimum wage), a career extending beyond age 60 significantly reduces pension wealth as a proportion of the discounted wage received during the extra year of work, imposing *de facto* a heavy "implicit tax" on working longer (Table 23, Panel A).[129] A similar phenomenon affects those whose careers extend beyond age 62 if they have already contributed for more than 40 years (including those earning the mean wage). In this case, the cut in the replacement rate to offset smaller contributions is reduced to 6 per cent, and it cannot be applied at all if the pension is a minimum benefit.[130] Despite these incentives, the number of persons taking early retirement under the general scheme has fallen for some years now, as the entitlement was confined to those who were contributing prior to 1967.[131] With the recent extension of the entitlement to early retirement regardless of the date of their first contribution to social security and the decrease of reduction coefficients applied to pensions, there is a risk that early retirement will start growing again.

As in many other countries, the legislation entitles workers in dangerous or health-taxing occupations (like seamen and miners) to retire at 60 with no reduction of pension. However, most of the persons covered by the other special schemes, like farm workers and the self-employed, do not have this entitlement, with the result that their mean age at retirement is close to the statutory age (Table 19). By contrast, the provisions concerning early retirement for central government employees are very generous, since these persons may retire at 60 without any penalty if they have contributed for at least 30 years (Box 6). Since 1984, the number of early retirees has amounted to about a third of the number of civil servants that entered the pension scheme.

Up to the mid-80s, permanent invalidity pensions were often used as a means of encouraging early retirement to offset job cuts due to restructuring. Since 1985 the eligibility criteria for these pensions have been tightened such that the share of invalidity pension expenditure in total pension expenditure has decreased to less than 12 per cent in 2000, which is not particularly high relative to other countries.[132] In the schemes for domestic employees, farm workers and the self-employed, most of the new holders of invalidity pensions are aged over 55 and therefore closer to retirement age. This suggests, given that invalidity

Table 23. **Implicit tax rates for an extra year of work**

Per cent

A. Early retirement

Retirement age	Years of contribution	Replacement rate[1]		Implicit tax rate[2]	
		Minimum wage	Average wage	Minimum wage	Average wage
61	30	85.0	54.3	81.3	−48.2
62	31	85.0	63.3	81.9	−59.7
63	32	85.0	70.9	82.6	−29.0
64	33	85.0	78.8	79.2	−21.6
65	34	87.1	86.9	61.9	−13.3
61	36	85.0	63.9	81.3	−21.7
62	37	85.0	70.1	81.9	−13.1
63	38	85.0	77.2	77.6	−16.5
64	39	85.0	83.0	80.1	11.3
65	40	88.8	88.7	43.7	20.0
61	41	85.0	67.4	81.3	−5.3
62	42	85.0	72.8	81.9	2.2
63	43	85.0	78.1	75.9	9.9
64	44	85.0	83.4	81.4	17.8
65	45	88.8	88.7	44.1	25.9

B. Career extension beyond age 65 without exemption from social insurance contributions[3]

Retirement age	Years of contribution	Replacement rate[1]	Implicit tax rate[2]
65	30	79.8	..
66	31	81.6	69.7
65	35	88.7	..
66	36	88.7	97.8

C. Career extension beyond age 65 assuming exemption from social insurance contributions[3]

65	35	88.7	..
66	36	88.7	69.5

1. On gross wages.
2. The implicit tax rate is estimated as the ratio between the change in pension wealth corresponding to an extra year of work and the discounted last salary. An extra year of working life causes a change in pension wealth, on the one hand, from the increased contributions made and the shorter period the pension is received (negative effect) and, on the other hand, from the higher pension if the replacement rate increases (positive effect). A positive value for the tax rate indicates that the pension wealth is reduced and shows this decrease as a share of wages (discounted) received during the extra year of work.
3. Average wage.
Source: OECD.

pensions are generous, that they are still a means of bringing forward the retirement of these workers.[133]

Several other arrangements permit early retirement in the event of corporate restructuring. Most retirements in such cases are the subject of negotiated agreements between the social partners under redundancy procedures (*Expediente de regulación de empleo*). The agreements, whose features vary, concern financing of the unemployment benefit supplement and social insurance contributions of older workers so as to give them an adequate level of income when retiring. These arrangements, generally used by big firms, are financed by a combination of redundancy payments (deferred payment), a contribution from the firm and, in some cases, government aid.[134] The total number of persons using these advance retirement arrangements has declined since the mid 90s as business conditions have improved.[135] However, a future recession would probably cause that number to rebound.

The pension system, which includes some elements that favour early retirement, did not provide incentives to extend activity beyond age 65 until March 2001. The recent measures should eliminate this problem to some extent by allowing the receipt of a partial pension while continuing to work, which was until now very difficult for most regimes. The conditions under which this will be possible are still to be defined, but they will allow for a progressive transition to retirement. Moreover, the measures adopted in March 2001 include the exemption of social contributions for those that continue working after 65. However, despite this measure, the way pensions are calculated implies that it is still very costly to continue work beyond age 65 for someone who has contributed for 35 years (Table 23, Panels B and C).

The private system of supplementary pensions is still little developed

In Spain the private pension system acts as a top-up to the public system. Since 1988 firms and individuals can take out voluntary pension plans with financial institutions. The private system is one of funded pension schemes and therefore not directly affected by the process of population ageing. However, it is not very developed as yet. In 1999 the estimated volume of private savings in the different private pension plans was about 20 per cent of GDP, of which half was for corporate contracts covering 2.6 million persons (18 per cent of total employment). But the savings accumulated in corporate insurance represent a real supplementary pension system only in a limited number of sectors, notably the big-business sectors of finance, energy and telecommunications.[136]

The development of private supplementary pension schemes was one of the recommendations of the Toledo Pact of 1995 and the authorities introduced tax incentives. These measures, which were strengthened in June 2000, are particularly advantageous for investing in private pension funds. Taxation of benefits is deferred and, if they are used in a corporate plan, entitle workers to a supplementary pension even if they leave the company. A process of externalisation whereby the financial liabilities associated with the pension agreements are removed from corporate balance sheets has also been set in motion to guarantee the entitlements of employees in the event of business failure (Annex VII). The externalisation process should favour the development of the market of private pension funds, which is regulated by the Ministry of Economy. Growth of these funds has been very pronounced since the mid-90s.[137] However, they have largely concerned individual contracts rather than corporate contracts.[138] In 1999 the number of corporate pension funds covered less than 3 per cent of total employment.

There are several reasons why the favourable tax treatment and high yields of pension funds have not resulted in a more rapid expansion of corporate contracts, especially in SMEs, which account for 80 per cent of dependent employment in Spain.[139] First there are the practical difficulties involved in setting up a pension plan for a small firm: considerable paperwork, lack of information and negotiation costs. Then there are other undesirable elements from the employer's standpoint. Once the pension plan has been negotiated, it has to be systematically applied to the entire staff of the firm and supervised by a board on which representatives of employees form the majority. This means that employers have limited oversight of fund management and investment policy. From the employees' standpoint, one obstacle to a more rapid development of pension plans in SMEs is the relatively low level of average wages, which leaves little room for a contribution additional to the social security charge. And the high replacement rate of most pensions in the public system is not conducive to the purchase of a supplementary pension. In these circumstances, private pension plans are attractive essentially to high-wage earners eligible for public pensions with low replacement rates.

Family assistance is helping to limit poverty among the elderly

One of the essential questions regarding the pension system is whether it satisfactorily performs its primary function of protecting the elderly against the risk of poverty. Since one third of all pensions are minimum benefits ranging from 20 to 30 per cent of the average wage, a large proportion of retirees should in theory be below the poverty line (50 per cent of the median income). But the poverty problem, on which there is no detailed recent information, has to be put into perspective. A great deal depends on the type of household in which older persons live. In Spain, as in Portugal, Ireland and Italy, the great majority of pensioners live with their children, and this informal assistance from families provides older persons with living standards similar to those of the rest of the population (Table 24). At the beginning of the 90s the poverty rate among persons living in households with pensioners was about 13½ per cent, a level only slightly above the average in other countries (Hauser, 1999). The poverty rate is higher among the oldest pensioners, most of whom are women.[140] In 1998 the old-age pensions of persons aged over 85 were 30 per cent lower than those of persons aged 65-69.

Given the prominence of minimum pensions in the old-age income support system, the question of raising them is the subject of recurrent debate.

Table 24. **Comparison of pensioners' income in selected OECD countries**
In the early 1990s, per cent

	Pensioners' household structure (% of total)			Ratio of the equivalent average income of persons in a pensioner household/non-pensioner household[1]	Ratio of the equivalent average income of women/men pensioners living alone[1]	Poverty rate in pensioner households[2]	
	Single	Couples without children	Other			Total	Where the head of household is aged over 75
Spain	**8.3**	**25.8**	**65.9**	**97.2**	**80.2**	**13.6**	**15.2**
Belgium	18.6	46.4	35.0	91.5	76.0	7.2	9.0
Denmark	40.8	52.1	7.0	81.5	94.9	4.1	6.2
France	25.2	44.1	30.6	100.7	78.1	11.9	13.3
Germany[3]	33.5	44.2	22.3	92.8	82.9	9.5	9.5
Ireland	15.3	15.9	68.8	89.2	112.6	10.8	5.6
Italy	20.5	30.2	49.2	79.0	84.4	17.6	15.2
Luxembourg	22.2	37.6	40.3	98.0	79.4	8.5	7.6
Netherlands	32.4	53.6	14.0	100.6	83.5	3.9	4.0
Portugal	10.0	34.0	56.0	72.2	64.3	27.5	42.7
United Kingdom	28.4	44.5	27.1	79.6	85.1	23.3	30.4
Canada	23.4	39.2	37.3	97.6	91.2	7.2	4.0
United States	22.9	41.0	36.1	99.9	83.4	20.5	21.8
Average of above countries	23.2	39.1	37.7	90.8	84.3	12.7	14.2

1. The equivalent average income is calculated by dividing the income of the household by the sum of the equivalent weights for all the household members. This weighting system counts 1 for the head of the household, 0.7 for each other member aged 14 or above and 0.5 for younger children. A pensioner household is defined as one in which the head is aged 55 or over and in which at least one member receives a pension. Most of the data used were collected in the context of the LIS project (Luxembourg Income Survey).
2. The poverty level is set at 50 per cent of the equivalent average income.
3. West Germany.
Source: Hauser (1999).

Management of basic income support is complicated by a number of factors. First, the existence of two minimum pensions, contributory and non-contributory, makes it necessary to ensure that their respective levels are such that workers will be encouraged to contribute. A second difficulty arises from the fact that contributory pensions are managed by central government through the INSS (*Instituto Nacional de Seguridad Social*), while non-contributory pensions are managed jointly by the State, which finances them through taxes, and the Autonomous Communities, which are responsible for social assistance. But the competencies of these two levels of government are not clearly defined as regards fixing the amount of non-contributory pensions. In fact, a conflict of competence arose in 2000 in this matter, which provides an example of fiscal irresponsibility that can arise with the decentralisation process. Some of the Autonomous Communities insisted on a larger increase in non-contributory pensions than the one initially set by the central government. The result was a process of leap-frogging that led to a steep rise (6.1 per cent) in these benefits and, as a result, in contributory minimum pensions as well. It therefore appears necessary for the legislature to clarify the responsibilities of the different levels of government and to impose consistency between the setting and financing of these pensions.[141]

The elderly receive most of their care informally through the family

In the face of growing demand for health and social services...

As in other OECD countries the demand for social and health services in Spain is rising as the population ages. The consumption of medical services and pharmaceutical products is highest among the elderly. In 1998, health spending by persons aged over 65 years amounted to 44 per cent of the national total, although this group represented only 19 per cent of the population covered (INSALUD, 1999). Assuming that expenditure ratios by age group, which are similar to the OECD average, remain unchanged, the impact of ageing can be expected to lead to an upward creep of ¼ to ½ percentage point in the growth rate of medical spending each year between 2000 and 2050. Considerable uncertainties surround, however, the evolution of the health expenditure ratio by age group.[142] Apart from strictly medical aspects, the problems associated with dependency tend to increase with age,[143] and often relate to difficulties in performing simple everyday tasks such as household chores or personal grooming and hygiene. The profile of care needs is shifting as life expectancy lengthens, and the medical component is increasing in comparison with other, purely social needs. At the end of the 90s, nearly 1.5 million people aged over 65 were in need of long-term care, and one million of these, or 16 per cent of the entire age group (INE, 2000) were severely or totally incapacitated. This rate rises with age and is frequently twice as high after 75 years. The rising proportion of people aged over 80, which stood at

3.7 per cent in 2000 and could reach 11 per cent by 2050, will therefore exert heavy pressure on the demand for social services.

> ... *the availability of social services is inadequate...*

Social services and medical care are organised in different ways. Health care services are universally available, and are essentially public and free.[144] The management of public health expenditure has been partly decentralised in recent years.[145] Health spending represented 5.4 per cent of GDP in 2000, which is relatively low in international comparison. Because coverage by the national health system is universal, a person's age has little bearing on access to such services. Pensioners are exempt from "user charges" when purchasing drugs, and medical care is thus completely free. The fact that drugs are freely available tends to encourage excessive spending (Chapter II).

The management of social services, on the other hand, has been completely decentralised, and now lies with the Autonomous Communities or other local entities, each with its own social assistance networks and facilities (long-term residences, day centres, at-home help, etc.). It is the local authorities, for example, that set the fees for publicly run residences for the elderly, and these generally take account of an applicant's financial and family situation, age and degree of disability. There is little information available on the average share paid directly by users of these public social services. In recent years, efforts have been made under the Gerontology Plan 1991-2000 to provide increased social assistance to the elderly: between 1988 and 1998, the number of places in old-age residences rose from 2.2 to 3.2 per cent of the over-65 population, thanks mainly to private facilities. Telecare programmes and day centres have also been developed. Yet these new facilities have been insufficient to meet demand, and have failed to achieve the objectives set in the plan, in particular with respect to non-institutionalised care.[146] The overall supply, private and public, covers only a portion of current demand. The rate of coverage of social services for the over-65 population is only half the OECD average in the case of residences, and a fifth in the case of home help (Table 25). Moreover there are major disparities between regions, despite central government efforts to co-ordinate certain social programmes.[147] The coverage ratio, in terms of places in old-age residences relative to the over-65 population, varies across the Communities by a factor of 1 to 3, and by as much as 1 to 6 when it comes to home-help services (Observatorio de Personas Mayores, 2000).

Most old-age residences are private (60 per cent of the total), and their organisation poses a number of problems. In some cases, private services are not up to adequate quality standards (in terms of medical attention, living conditions, etc.). This situation would seem to reflect poor co-ordination between the local authorities and private providers in terms of certifying social centres and enforcing minimum quality standards.[148] In most cases, however, private services are of

Table 25.   **Comparison of old-age care and health systems**

	Expenditure on services for the elderly[1] as a % of GDP, 1997	% of population aged 65 and over, 1995		Expenditure on health as a % of GDP, 1998	
		In institutions[2]	Receiving formal help at home[3]	Total	Public
Spain	**0.21**	**2.8**	**2**	**7.1**	**5.4**
Austria	0.24	4.9	24	8.2	5.8
Belgium	..	6.4	5	8.8	7.9
Denmark	1.72	7.0	20	8.3	6.8
Finland	0.80	5.3 to 7.6	14	6.9	5.3
France	0.64	6.5	6	9.6	7.3
Germany	0.70	6.8	10	10.6	7.9
Ireland	0.19	5.0	4	6.4	4.8
Italy	0.20	3.9	3	8.4	5.7
Netherlands	0.25	8.8 (2.7 NH)[4]	12	8.6	6.0
Portugal	0.14	..	..	7.8	5.2
Sweden	3.40	8.7	11	8.4	7.0
United Kingdom	..	5.1	6	6.7	5.6
Australia	0.25	6.8	12	8.5	5.9
Canada	..	6.2 to 7.5	17	9.5	6.6
Japan	0.09	6.0 (3.0 NH)[4]	5	7.6	6.0
Norway	2.94	6.6	17	8.9	7.4
United States	0.04	5.7	16	13.6	6.1
Average of above countries:[5]					
EU	0.77	6.0	10	8.1	6.2
OECD	0.79	6.1	11	8.6	6.3

1. Residential care, home-help services, day care and rehabilitation services.
2. Estimates may vary according to the concept chosen for institutions (sheltered housing, homes for the elderly, nursing homes). Normally, the concept described should include only staffed homes. For Denmark the concept of older persons refers mostly to over 67 year-olds.
3. Older persons receiving formal help at home, including district nursing, and help with activities of daily living.
4. Some of the residential accommodation is provided within hospitals. The data in parentheses refer to nursing homes (NH) only.
5. The averages shown are purely indicative since the data are not strictly comparable across countries.
Source: OECD Social Expenditure database and OECD *Health Data 2000*; OECD (1999), A *Caring World. The New Social Policy Agenda.*

good quality, but their cost is too high for the majority of the population, while the availability of public services is limited, and reserved primarily for the poorest. The average monthly cost of a post in a private residence is roughly 2½ times the average monthly pension and must be entirely financed by the user. The Gerontology Plan called for a pension supplement after age 80, because dependency tends to increase after that age, but this was never implemented. Middle classes, therefore, have a problem of access to private social services. Given the prospect of increased demand for such services in the future, pressures are likely to emerge for extending the coverage of public social services.

... and it implies heavy reliance on informal family care

This shortage of supply means that much of the burden falls upon family caregivers, who meet more than 60 per cent of demand. Traditionally, it was women who provided care to elderly dependants. The number of persons performing informal social assistance tasks is estimated at 1.7 million, and more than 80 per cent of these are women aged 45 to 64 years, a factor that has certainly made it more difficult for them to enter the labour market. With fewer children in a position to look after their parents, this reliance on informal assistance from family members, and from women in particular, is increasingly being called into question, as care requirements become more complex, the age of dependants continues to rise, and more women are entering the workforce.

The structure of supply is inadequate in terms of services provided

The shortcomings of the health and social services networks frequently lead to inappropriate use of health care services to meet social needs, and *vice versa*. Keeping chronically dependent elderly persons in hospital is inefficient from both the social and the financial viewpoint, since this costs five to six times more than placing them in residential institutions. In addition, the underdeveloped state of non-institutionalised care (in the form of at-home help, day-care centres or outpatient clinics, telecare, etc.) tends to inflate demand for admission to institutions. Such placements are often highly unsatisfactory, not only from the viewpoint of elderly people themselves, who would prefer to stay at home or with their family, but also from the financial viewpoint. Annual costs in a public residence, at between ESP 1.8 and 2.4 million in 1999, are about three times as high as those for day centres (Observatorio de Personas Mayores, 2000). And they are perhaps ten times greater than providing at-home assistance, and as much as 50 times the cost of telecare services. It is, thus, important, to improve the co-ordination of social and health services and to place greater stress on non-institutional care to meet demand in a cost-effective manner.

The authorities are considering two different approaches for encouraging the development of a financially sound private system of services. The first is based on a system of vouchers, similar to those in place in other countries, and this is now on trial in selected Communities. These vouchers provide a right to private social services, for which the financing is shared, according to a flexible formula, between the user, his family and the public sector. A second approach involves the establishment of private insurance plans for care to the elderly. The risk covered is a complex one, however: it is not a financially defined benefit, but rather a service in kind. The use of insurance of this type is likely to be limited to the better-off groups, unless it is supported with sufficient tax incentives.

The impact of ageing on public finances

Different sets of projections have been produced recently to gauge the impact of ageing on the public pension system and, more broadly, on public finances. Most of these studies point to financial viability problems over the long term. This is the case, in particular, with the projections prepared by the Spanish experts using their national model that fed into both ECOFIN and OECD's work on ageing (OECD, 2001). Such projections, co-ordinated by the OECD, are available for several countries, on the basis of homogeneous macroeconomic and demographic assumptions, and thus permit international comparisons.[149] In the case of Spain, the data cover contributory earnings-related pensions (including those for central government employees), but they do not take into account the impact of ageing on social and medical spending. The results suggest that pension expenditures should remain fairly close to their current level of about 10 per cent of GDP until 2020-25, when they will jump sharply, reaching more than 17 per cent of GDP by 2050 (Figure 29). This rise in expenditure by nearly 8 percentage points of GDP in 50 years, with most of it concentrated in the second half of this period, is much steeper than that projected for other OECD countries (except Norway), where it averages between 3 and 4 percentage points (OECD, 2001). Assuming that expenditure ratios by age group remain stable at their current level, estimates suggest that the ageing-driven increase in public health spending will add ¾ to 1½ per cent of GDP between 2000 and 2050. But this rough estimate does not include long-term care spending for the old, which could rise strongly as informal family help diminishes progressively. Available estimates for a number of OECD countries that will experience a milder demographic shock and that have a more developed infrastructure for social services than Spain indicate that, on average, the total health expenditure (including long-term care) related to ageing might increase by about 3 per cent of GDP by 2050.

In the scenario examined, average output growth is estimated at 1.8 per cent per year for the next 50 years. According to the relatively optimistic assumptions made about labour force participation and unemployment rates, the employment/total population ratio should be slightly higher by 2050. This would in effect erase the negative impact that the ageing process has on growth of GDP per capita over the next half-century. Yet these projections highlight the magnitude of the intergenerational transfers if the current parameters of the pension system remain unchanged. Pensions are much higher than they would be in an actuarially neutral system, and this implies the relative impoverishment of future working generations.[150] The internal rate of return on pensions, in excess of 4 per cent, is much higher than potential long-term economic growth. Recent studies based on a generational accounting approach show that the debt implicit in the pension system, and which future generations will inherit, could reach 176 per cent of GDP in present value terms (Bonin *et al.*, 1999).[151]

Figure 29. **Pension expenditure projections**
Per cent of GDP

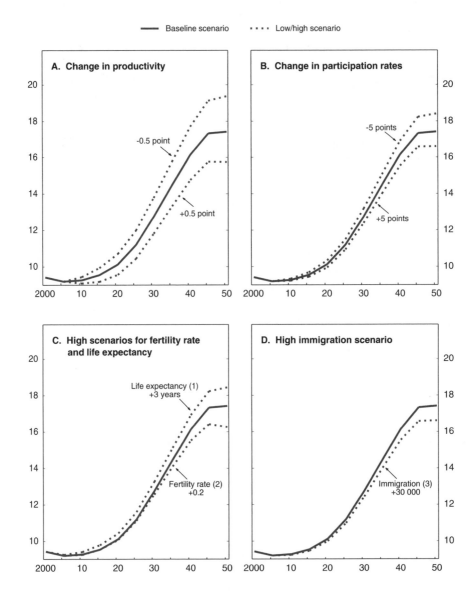

—— Baseline scenario   ·· ·· Low/high scenario

1. Progressive increase in life expectancy by 2050 (+4 years for men and +2 years for women).
2. Progressive rise in the fertility rate from 1.5 (baseline) to 1.7 as from 2025.
3. Increase of net immigration from 60 000 people a year (baseline) to 90 000 from 2010 onwards.
Source: OECD (2001), *OECD Economic Outlook* No. 69 and data supplied by national experts.

In the projections prepared by national experts, the ratio of public debt to GDP would not be higher in 2050 than in 2000 (around 60 per cent). This favourable result is due to the assumption that the primary surplus of 3½ per cent of GDP, excluding the pension system, will be maintained over the next 50 years.[152] If pensions did not grow, such a surplus would imply an accumulation of assets of 225 per cent of GDP between 2000 and 2050. But this increase of assets will be offset by higher pension expenditure, whose negative effects on debt accumulation should continue at a very rapid pace beyond 2050. Moreover, the hypothesis of maintaining a high primary surplus excluding pensions seems too optimistic, since it does not take into account strong pressures on health and social expenditure in the future. It also does not consider possible future reductions in taxes and social security contributions as the debt falls and the public accounts are in surplus until 2025. In any case, this scenario illustrates the important role of a strict budgetary policy to limit the impact of ageing on the public debt.

An analysis of the determinants of pension expenditure in the scenario prepared by national experts shows the key role played by the rising old-age dependency ratio, particularly after 2025 (Table 26). The improvement in the employment rate resulting from reduced unemployment and increased female participation only offsets one-quarter of the higher pension spending caused by the demographic shock. These projections appear quite optimistic, however, because of the assumptions about the number of pensions and their average level relative to productivity (or real wages).[153] These two factors are projected to restrain the increase in pension expenditure relative to GDP over the next 50 years. Yet, the current system does not seem to guarantee such a moderate trend of pension spending. The rise in average pensions relative to real wages (or productivity) of recent decades is likely to continue, given the generous parameters of the pension system and the lengthening of contribution periods as unemployment declines and fewer people take early retirement.[154]

These projections are fairly similar to those found in the other available studies. All predict a limited increase in pension expenditure until 2025, followed by a rapid jump, varying between 4¾ and 6½ percentage points of GDP, in the period from 2025 to 2050 (Table 26, Panel B).[155] However, the discrepancies found between the different sets of projections, which reflect different demographic and macroeconomic assumptions, underline the uncertainties inherent in exercises of this type. For this reason sensitivity tests of the projections to alternative hypotheses have been carried out. The tests showed, for example, that if productivity rises by 0.5 percentage point per year more than in the central scenario, pension spending would be 1¾ percentage points of GDP lower at the 2050 horizon (Figure 29).[156] If the participation rate were 5 percentage points higher than in the central scenario, pension expenditure would be nearly 1 percentage point of GDP lower. With a more favourable demographic trend than projected, pension spending growth would also be reduced. Beyond the uncertainties that they illustrate,

Table 26.   **Components of pension expenditure until 2050**[1]
Percentage points

	1990-2000	2000-25	2025-50	2000-50
A. Central projections				
Change in the ratio of pension expenditure as a % of GDP	1.3	1.8	6.2	8.0
of which, contributions from:				
Dependency ratio	1.1	2.8	7.8	10.6
Employment rate	−0.6	−1.5	−1.1	−2.6
Number of pensions per person aged over 65	0.1	0.9	−1.6	−0.6
Ratio of average pensions to real wages	0.6	−0.6	0.6	−0.1
Residual effect[2]	0.1	0.1	0.5	0.7
B. Comparison with other studies				
Change in the ratio of pension expenditure as a % of GDP				
Jimeno (2000)[3]	..	1.4	6.5	7.9
Herce and Alonso-Meseguer (2000)[4]	..	1.6	4.7	6.3
Comisiones Obreras (2000)[5]	..	1.2	..	..
	1990	2000	2025	2050
Memorandum item				
Ratio of pension expenditure as a % of GDP	8.1	9.4	11.2	17.4

1. The components of projected pension expenditure as a percentage of GDP were calculated using the following formula:

$$\frac{\text{Pension}}{\text{GDP}} = \frac{\text{Number of pensions}}{\text{Population aged over 65}} \times \text{Dependency ratio} \times \frac{1}{\text{Employment rate}} \times \frac{\text{Average pension}}{\text{Average productivity}}$$

2. The components are calculated using a linear logarithmic formula that leaves a residual.
3. Projections based on the assumption that productivity will increase by 2.5 per cent annually and the ratio for average pension/productivity will remain constant.
4. Balance of the pension schemes and not expenditure as a percentage of GDP. Projections based on an annual 3 per cent productivity increase.
5. Projections based on an annual 2.5 per cent productivity increase.
Source: OECD (2001), "Fiscal implications of ageing: projections of age-related spending", OECD *Economic Outlook* No. 69, and OECD calculations based on data supplied by national experts.

these sensitivity tests show the relatively limited role of the factors influencing the projections when they are taken individually. On the other hand, they point to the important complementary role that policy can play, by inducing greater labour efficiency, increased immigration, higher labour force participation rates and a more successful reconciliation of family and working life.

The OECD has also produced simulations in order to measure the impact of changes to certain features of the general regime on the rate of return. The changes considered would bring the main parameters for pension calculation in line with those generally observed in other OECD countries. The results of the simulations are presented in Table 27. They show that increasing the number of contribution years from 35 to 40 for a full pension, changing the reference period for pension calculation so as to take account of earnings over an entire working life instead of just the final 15 years, and cutting the maximum replacement rate from

Table 27. **Implications of changing certain parameters of the general pension scheme**
For a career with 35 years of contributions and retirement at age 65, per cent of average wage

	Current system	Change in:			Combined changes (a)+(b)+(c)
		Contribution period (a)	Reference period (b)	Replacement rate (c)	
Maximum replacement ratio relative to the regulatory base	100	100	100	80	80
Contribution period for a full pension (years)	35	40	35	35	40
Reference period for the regulatory base (years)	Last 15	Last 15	Whole career	Last 15	Whole career
Replacement rate relative to the last wage	88.7	79.8	76.0	71.0	54.7
Internal rate of return	4.1	3.7	3.5	3.2	2.2
Memorandum item Average real GDP growth rate over 2000-50	1.8	..	..	..	..

Source: OECD.

100 to 80 per cent, would reduce the internal rate of return of the general scheme to around 2 per cent, or a level close to average potential growth over 2000-50. Moreover, as shown by other OECD work (OECD, 2001), increasing the effective age of retirement would also be quite effective for raising the financial viability of the pension system. Delaying the effective retirement age by two months would be equivalent to more than a 3 per cent reduction in average pensions.

The options for reform

Reforms are needed

Reforms are necessary to prepare Spain to cope with the consequences of population ageing. While it will come relatively late, only after 2020-25, the demographic shock will be particularly severe and pension schemes will run into serious financial difficulties. There will also be ageing-related pressures on health care expenditure and social services. Spain has enough time to introduce reforms gradually and let people adapt to them. No time should be wasted, however. The currently favourable situation of the pension schemes, even if continuing for a number of years, should not lead to illusions. Neither the 1997 social security reform nor the recent measures adopted in March 2001 have contributed to reduce the expected impact of ageing on the evolution of pension expenditure. However, by separating the funding sources for social programmes, the reform has served to clarify the social security accounts, and this will enhance the financial balance of the pension schemes over the next few years. Yet in the end it has merely transferred part of the burden of financing the foreseeable increases in health, pension and social assistance spending to other levels of government.

A sound fiscal policy is essential, but not enough by itself

A sound fiscal policy should be an important element of any plan for dealing with the problems stemming from the ageing process. In this respect, the pending introduction of a fiscal stability law, which will require a balanced budget at every level of government, and the recent creation of a social security reserve fund are steps in the right direction. Overall, the social security system should record surpluses until 2020-25. The reserve fund envisaged by the authorities is of limited size (about 1 per cent of GDP, *i.e.* a little more than one month's pension spending), but the fiscal stability law, if it is adopted, could bring about a significant reduction in public debt.[157] The strategy of reducing debt or building up assets before the demographic shock occurs might be part of the response to the problems linked with ageing. However, it cannot avoid bringing down the generosity of the pension system to a level which is consistent with the financing capacity of the economy in the long term. Moreover, this strategy carries a number of risks that may be difficult to guard against. These relate to the uncertainties of the budgeting process, where the time frame is limited and political considerations necessarily play a part. It is likely that, at times when the budget is in surplus and debt is declining, there will be strong pressures to raise the generosity of pension benefits or to reduce contributions. Such pressures have already occurred in the recent past. The funding of the reserve is unlikely to be automatic, because it will inevitably be linked to the budgetary trade-offs which will evolve over time. This represents an important limit of this approach. However, the Fiscal Stability Draft Law envisages automatic funding as a priority.

It will be difficult to avoid reducing the generosity of pensions...

Under these circumstances it will be difficult to avoid reducing the generosity of the pension system. The current parameters of the pension system are more generous than those in most OECD countries. The implicit rates of return that pensioners enjoy on their contributions exceed the long-run potential economic growth rate for coming decades. Even with the likelihood of higher employment rates offsetting in part the increase in the dependency ratio, public pension spending could rise by 8 percentage points of GDP by 2050. This increase could be still steeper if average pensions continue to grow faster than real wages. It is hardly feasible to raise contribution rates, because of the negative fallout this would have on the labour market. A revision of the pension system's parameters would therefore seem necessary to bring the parameters for calculating pensions in line with those of other countries. Some of the changes that might be made to this end would be to base pension calculations on lifelong occupational earnings, rather than those of the last 15 years, to increase the number of contribution years to obtain a full pension from 35 to 40 years, and to cut back the replacement rate from 100 to 80 per cent.

... which will have an impact on all schemes and require the harmonisation of their rules

Reducing the generosity of the pension system should not be limited to the general scheme but should extend to all schemes, including the one for central government employees. It would be desirable if the special regimes could be integrated gradually into the general scheme, as the Toledo Pact has in fact recommended. In the case of the public service regime, a harmonisation of the rules for financing and calculating pensions with those applying to private sector workers would help to clarify its financial situation and eliminate certain provisions that are very generous. Concerning the major special social security schemes (for farmers, the self-employed and domestic employees), the contribution bases and rates are lower than for the general scheme, which generates incentives to reduce contribution periods. There is little doubt that these special rules encourage work in the underground economy. Phasing them out would reduce the large transfers to some of these schemes and would reinforce the insurance function of the pension system. And for all schemes the possibility of combining widows' pensions with other pensions should be restricted and made subject to an income test. With the growing participation of women in the labour market, the cost of this option is likely to rise steadily.[158] Full inflation-indexing of pensions is also a problem when there is a negative shock, such as a large increase in oil prices. The system then protects pensioners from any adjustment of their incomes thus imposing an extra burden on public finances, as has happened with the 2001 Budget. Amendments to this indexing system should be considered.

Care must be taken, however, to ensure that a less generous pension system does not lead to greater poverty among the elderly. The high number of minimum pensions suggests that such a risk exists. Yet it must be remembered that the proportion of these pensions has declined in recent years. That trend should continue, as more women join the labour market and as unemployment falls. If more stringent rules are introduced gradually, increased accrual pension rights that agents will acquire with longer careers than in the past should offset their effect on pension levels. This would help ensure a more equitable distribution of income between the working and non-working population, in light of the economy's financing capacity.

Early retirement incentives should be eliminated, particularly for public servants...

A further set of measures should focus on developing incentives to encourage older workers to remain in the labour market. Delaying the effective retirement age would be effective in limiting the problems of public finances related to ageing. In addition, these measures could help avoid subsequent problems of poverty that could follow a reduction in the system's generosity. To this end, the financial incentives to early retirement and the disincentives to postponing retirement should be eliminated. Currently, low-wage earners and workers who have contributed for more than 40 years to the general scheme have an incentive to stop work before they are 65. This incentive was increased in March 2001 with the cut in the reduction coefficient of pensions in the case of early retirement. The incentives are even stronger for central government employees, who enjoy more generous early retirement rules than do other workers. Given that the possibility to take early retirement in the general scheme was expanded in March 2001, the gradual fall in early retirement recorded over the last years risks coming to an end. In the case of the central government and the general schemes, incentives in favour of early retirement should be reduced. The best option to do so would be to revise the pension formula so as to put pensions on an actuarially neutral basis. Also, steps should be taken to encourage labour market re-entry by the older unemployed, whose benefits are low but last until their retirement. Finally, early retirement rules for workers affected by corporate restructuring should be tightened. To the extent that retirements of this kind are in part financed with redundancy allowances, reducing such compensation as part of labour market reform would be a welcome way of reducing the risk that the system will be used more heavily in times of recession.

... and disincentives for older workers to stay in the workforce should be suppressed

Several measures have been recently adopted to encourage workers to remain at work beyond the legal age of retirement. The government has for instance decided to exempt totally those still working after age 65 from social contributions. While this exemption will raise the employability of older workers, it is unlikely that this would increase older workers' incomes enough to encourage them to extend their working life beyond age 65. In the absence of modifications to the current system of accumulating rights beyond the age of 65, which creates disincentives for older workers to stay in the workforce, the development of possibilities for a progressive transition to retirement beyond age 65, decided in March 2001, would however help to prolong peoples' working lives. But the details concerning this new possibility of combining a pension with earned income remain to be defined.

Thought should be given to strengthening the private pension system or to making it compulsory

Another option for dealing with the consequences of ageing would be to reinforce the private system of pre-funded pensions. As suggested by the Toledo

Pact, this system can play a useful complementary role to reinforce social protection, if it is developed in co-ordination with the public system. For one thing, it opens the possibility of diversifying the structure of "assets" underlying pension finance by broadening the proportion of financial assets, which will stimulate the development of capital markets. Encouraging private occupational plans would also enhance the collective bargaining process and could help relieve wage pressures, since a portion of pay increases could be negotiated in the form of higher pension rights.[159]

There are, however, a number of obstacles holding back the development of the private occupational pension system. Implementing a private system is difficult, especially for SMEs. Moreover, these supplementary plans seem to be of only limited appeal to workers with modest incomes. If the public system were made less generous, this would increase the incentive for workers to join such plans. Steps should also be taken to rebalance the boards that supervise these plans, on the basis of equal representation of employers and employees. Low-wage earners, however, are unlikely to accept the reduction in take-home pay that results from making voluntary contributions to a private pension plan. The authorities might consider making such plans a compulsory second pillar of the pension system. A stronger funded pillar would partly offset the reduced generosity of the public system, and would represent a useful measure that would make the pension system more flexible.

Achieving a higher participation rate within a less generous system

There are other reforms that could increase the economically active portion of the population over the longer term, and that could also help to resolve the economic problems linked with population ageing. Such measures could include an increase in immigration, and steps to reduce unemployment and increase the female presence in the labour market. Most of the pension expenditure projections incorporate assumptions of a higher employment rate. However, if these measures are to be effective over the long term, the system will have to be made less generous. Given the implicit high yields that the pension system is committed to pay future retirees on their contributions, in the absence of reform these measures will have only a temporary effect and will merely postpone and ultimately worsen the problem of pension financing.[160]

Higher immigration is one possibility, but it has major limitations

Of all the possible approaches to increasing the employment rate, increased immigration is no doubt the most difficult to handle. A significant jump in the number of immigrants is likely to bring with it political and social problems.[161] In addition, economic policy has only a limited impact on the structure of the immigrant population. Nor is it possible to control the rate at which immigrants may return to their home country. Since Spain is a signatory of the Schengen agreement, secondary migration within the European Union makes it also difficult to achieve precise objectives with this kind of measure.

Better family services would increase female participation in the labour market

The development of infrastructure and facilities to meet the needs of families, such as kindergartens, day-care centres and social services that can help them to reconcile the demands of family and working life would be desirable for increasing the female participation rate. One obstacle to the accessibility of such services is their high cost, given that the purchasing power of families with young children is often limited. A private system co-financed by the public sector, for instance, through a voucher system, could help to overcome this obstacle. In addition, the labour market entry of women could be accelerated by deeper labour market reforms that would reduce structural unemployment, by more flexible part-time contracts, but also by a further strengthening of social services for dependant elderly, still provided informally by families. Improving economic conditions, particularly labour market opportunities for youth would also help to restore confidence in the future, which is a necessary condition for the revival of fertility rates which have been very low in recent years.

Appropriate social services for the aged need to be provided

With fewer children in a position to take care of their parents, with old age care becoming increasingly complex, and with ever more women joining the labour force, the informal mechanisms of caring for the elderly are being called increasingly into question. As the family role diminishes, it is important to raise the availability of social services. Preventive programmes for postponing and reducing the intensity of dependency should certainly be encouraged in order to restrain the demand for such services. Yet it can hardly be doubted that such demand will rise sharply. Greater availability of social services to the aged will produce efficiency gains in comparison to the current, essentially family-based organisation of such services.

Priority should be given to non-institutionalised care. It is important to prevent the growing demand for these services from translating into higher budget costs through the persistence of an inappropriate supply structure that encourages placement of the elderly in residential care. Regarding those in need of institutionalised care, the lack of sufficient residences or their high price might lead to an increased but inadequate use of much more expensive hospital institutions. Better co-ordination between social and health services (through a one-stop system) would be useful. A further question that must be addressed has to do with making social services available at affordable prices, given the limited resources of older people. Experiments with vouchers that allow a flexible mix of public and private funding, as well as the development of private insurance systems for social services, should be pursued. A specific social contribution might be introduced to protect the elderly from the risk of dependency, as has been done in other countries such as Germany. However, it is important to ensure that contributions are set at an adequate level, to avoid long-term financial viability problems. It is also important to ensure that services are available on an equitable basis in terms of their quality, wherever people may live. This will require greater co-operation among administrations.

The evolution of the pension system should be monitored regularly

An entire set of complementary measures will be required to deal with the consequences of ageing (Box 7). What is at stake is to ensure that the elderly have sufficient incomes, while respecting the financial constraints imposed by long-term production capacity. Measures to maintain a fair distribution of income in the future between the working and the non-working population will be needed. These must be supplemented by efforts to strengthen economic growth. Here, apart from policies to encourage higher employment, structural reforms to stimulate productivity would help to offset the negative impact of the demographic shock. The development of a private, funded pension system, complementary to and integrated with the public system, would also add flexibility to the overall pension system and would deepen capital markets. There is little doubt about the need for such changes and the direction they should take, and a prompt and determined commitment to reform is called for. The scope of any future reform is however subject to uncertainty because of the long time horizon involved. This is why the situation of the pension systems should remain subject to a regular review, for example every five years, as suggested in the Toledo Pact.

Box 7.   **Maintaining prosperity in an ageing society: recommendations
for Spain**

Reduce the public pension system's generosity and pursue fiscal consolidation

The demographic shock that Spain will face in the years after 2020 will be intense. The 1997 social security reform and the recent measures adopted in March 2001 have done little to reduce the expected impact of this shock on pension expenditure growth, which is very likely to be steeper than in other OECD countries. Moreover, there will also be pressure on health and social services spending. The authorities should consider the following measures:

– Reduce the generosity of the public pension system by bringing it in line with the pension calculation rules used in other countries. Following the OECD's calculation, this could mean: calculating pensions on the basis of lifelong occupational earnings, and not on the last 15 years; increasing the number of contribution years for a full pension from 35 to 40 years; and reducing the replacement rate from 100 to 80 per cent.

– Reduce the generosity of all pension schemes, including that for central government employees. These schemes should be gradually brought within the general system, which would imply harmonising their financing rules.

– Restrict the option of cumulating widows' benefits with other pensions, by introducing a means test.

– Pursue a sound fiscal policy that will reduce the public debt before the demographic shock occurs. The pending introduction of a fiscal stability law, which will require a balanced budget at each level of government, and the recent creation of a social security reserve fund are steps in the right direction.

**Eliminate financial incentives to early retirement and disincentives
to postponing retirement**

– Revise pension calculations for all the regimes on the basis of an actuarially neutral system that takes account of long-term economic growth prospects. This will imply a downward revision of the reduction coefficient of pensions in the case of early retirement for low income workers and those with a long contribution period.

– Restrict early retirement options related to corporate restructuring, by reducing redundancy allowances, as part of a broader labour market reform. Controls on the abuse of disability pensions could also be stepped up.

– Review the current system of pension right accrual beyond age 65, so as to remove financial disincentives to remaining in the workforce.

Improve employment opportunities for older workers

– Give greater priority to preserving the human capital and qualifications of older workers. Incentives for part-time work could also help keep these people in the workforce after age 65.

Box 7.   **Maintaining prosperity in an ageing society: recommendations for Spain** (*cont.*)

Diversify retirement income by encouraging private mechanisms

– Consider making a minimum contribution to the second pillar of the pension system compulsory.

Adopt effective regulations for pension funds

– Concerning the regulatory framework for the second-pillar pension plans currently in place, put pension supervisory boards on a basis of equal representation for employers and employees.

Expand the availability of social services providing care for the elderly

– Expand the supply of social services, with priority given to the promotion of non-institutionalised care, in order to avoid a sharp rise in budgetary costs. Co-ordination should also be strengthened between social and health services (with the introduction of a one-stop system).

– Develop a voucher system, with a flexible public-private financing mix, to ensure that social services are available at affordable prices. Private insurance for social services could also be encouraged by way of tax incentives.

– Ensure that quality care is available equitably to the entire population, wherever people live; this will require greater co-operation among administrations.

– Promote preventive programmes of geriatric care, with a view to postponing and reducing the intensity of dependency.

Establish a strategic framework

– An entire set of well-articulated complementary measures will be needed to cope with the consequences of ageing. Measures to ensure a fairer distribution of income between the working and non-working populations should be taken to supplement efforts to strengthen and maintain long-term economic growth. Such action could include measures to increase immigration, reduce unemployment and raise workforce participation by women, but they will not be effective in the long run unless pension generosity is decreased. Pension reform must also be linked to the development of social services for the elderly. A prompt and determined commitment to reform is called for. Given the uncertainties over the exact scope of the steps needed, the situation of the pension system should remain subject to regular review, for example every five years.

Notes

1. The growth differential with the euro area was 1½ percentage points between 1997 and 1999 and ¾ percentage point in 2000.

2. The decline in motor vehicle registrations was accentuated in late 2000 by the government's announcement that it would increase tax relief for the replacement of old cars and for large families as of January 2001. A large number of households is likely to have postponed their purchases as a result.

3. The wealth effect linked to the development of financial markets seems relatively weak in Spain, however, given the small share of household wealth held in the form of stock market investments (about 15 per cent). Also, this effect was probably offset by the increased value of their real estate holdings, their main source of household wealth. In 2000 property values rose by about 15 per cent. Housing prices in real terms climbed back to their 1991 levels, after falling steeply in the first half of the 1990s.

4. The swiftness of this deceleration surprised most analysts. Many observers thought that the investment slowdown indicated by the national accounts in the course of the year reflected estimation errors and that the figures would be scaled up substantially in the last quarter, but this was not the case.

5. Liberalisation of the communications and electricity sectors and the decline in energy costs until mid-1999 were other contributory factors.

6. The loss of competitiveness *vis-à-vis* the euro area is perceptible if the indicators used are labour cost and export prices in manufacturing industry, due to the continuing positive inflation differential with the euro area average. It is not perceptible if producer prices are used, these having risen more moderately.

7. According to social security figures, the increase in employment was 4½ per cent at the end of 2000 and the beginning of 2001, compared with 5½ per cent a year earlier.

8. See also Chapter II of the previous *Survey*, which presents the main aspects of the 1997 labour market reform. According to the National Institute of Employment (INEM), the number of subsidised employment contracts fell by 18 per cent in 2000, compared with a rise of 23 per cent in 1999.

9. The decrease in the proportion of temporary employment was more marked in industry (–3.4 points) and construction (–2.6 points) than in agriculture (–1.2 points) and in services (–1.1 points). In the government sector, there was actually an increase.

10. According to INEM's unemployment figures for the beginning of 2001, the decrease in joblessness was 3 per cent as against 7 per cent at the beginning of 2000 and over 10 per cent in 1998 and 1999.

11. The group of people with secondary or higher education represented 71.5 per cent of total unemployment in 2000.

12. The problems of productivity measurement were discussed in the previous *Survey* of Spain. The difficulties are reduced when using the employment statistics of the national accounts, which adjust the statistical breaks and discrepancies of coverage to be found in the data of the labour force surveys.

13. Productivity growth in Spain has also been lower in the present expansionary phase (0.8 per cent between 1995 and 2000) than in the previous one (1.7 per cent between 1987 and 1991) (Balmaseda *et al.*, 2000).

14. Construction, where employment has risen most in recent years, is the sector where productivity has actually fallen, presumably owing to the recruitment of low-skilled labour. According to the national accounts, productivity in this sector is also about 30 per cent lower than in the rest of the economy.

15. Corporate profits are calculated here as a residual. Thus they also include income of small businesses and other non-wage income.

16. The European Commission's consumer survey shows an above-average increase in inflation expectations during 2000 in Spain relative to other EU countries.

17. There is some difference between the nominal wage growth figures contained in the national accounts, which have been used in the analysis above, and those derived from surveys, which indicate more moderate rises. According to the survey on employee compensation, the results of which are published later than the other statistics, there has been no acceleration of average wages owing to the lower levels of pay awarded to new employees. However, the data from surveys and statistics on collective agreements have a narrower coverage than the national accounts data.

18. Productivity growth in industry has not been stronger than in the rest of the economy over the last five years in Spain. As a result, the negative differential in productivity growth with other euro area countries is probably even more pronounced in the industry sector than for the economy as a whole.

19. The fall in interest payments can be included among the structural factors as it reflects the permanent elimination of risk premia on interest rates due to the sounder economic conditions achieved prior to joining the euro area.

20. Monthly data of the central government budget, on a basis consistent with the national accounts, have been regularly published since 1999.

21. UMTS receipts have been factored out of the 2000 Budget figures for the purposes of this comparison.

22. The importance of the effect of interest charge reduction in the fiscal consolidation process is confirmed by the authorities, who estimate the saving achieved between 1996 and 2000 at ESP 1 200 billion or about 1.2 per cent of GDP. Between 1996 and 2000 the average life of the public debt increased by two years to its present length of 5.7 years, whilst the average rate of interest on that debt was reduced by nearly 2½ points to 5.7 per cent.

23. In 2000 general government consumption spending was equivalent to 17 per cent of GDP, less than the euro area average (20 per cent) and less than in the United Kingdom (18.5 per cent). As in the United States, public employment represented some 14 per cent of total employment in 2000, down by 2 percentage points since 1995.

24. The ratio of public investment to GDP, which stood at 3.3 per cent in 2000, is higher than the euro area average (2.5 per cent) and similar to the ratio in the United States.

This comparatively high level of public investment to improve the country's infrastructure is partly financed by large transfers from the European Union.

25. According to the government, the income tax reform has given taxpayers an aggregate relief of ESP 800 billion (0.8 per cent of GDP). The positive effect of increased activity, estimated at 0.5 point of GDP in 1999 which would correspond to the creation of 60 000 jobs, partly offset the cost of the tax cuts by reducing it to ESP 540 billion (0.55 per cent of GDP).

26. The apparent elasticity of indirect taxes with respect to GDP and private consumption was more than 1½ between 1998 and 2000.

27. The decentralisation process is continuing in 2001 with the transfer of competence for non-university education and justice from the State to the Autonomous Communities.

28. The projected growth of receipts from social security contributions in 2001, as compared with the 2000 Budget, is over 8 per cent. However, the growth of these receipts in 2000 was much more than expected. Relative to last year's outturns, the increase expected in 2001 is therefore only of the order of 4 per cent. This year, nominal per capita wages are expected to grow by 3 to 4 per cent. In the first quarter of 2001 employment was up by more than 4½ per cent according to the social security registers.

29. Strict checks will be kept on certain types of expenditure, such as public consumption of pharmaceutical products (see Chapter II). Monthly monitoring of ministries' budgets was also introduced this year.

30. The increase in this expenditure item is likely to be even larger because of increased pension payments. Pensions, which are indexed to headline inflation, have already been adjusted to catch up with the inflation overrun in 2000 and the same will happen in 2001.

31. According to the OECD's Interlink model, the public expenditure multiplier is estimated at 0.5 in the case of Spain, assuming fixed exchange and nominal interest rates. The value of this multiplier is similar to that obtained for the average of the other euro area countries.

32. According to the Stability Programme, the fall in tax revenue as a result of the reform would be 0.3 per cent of GDP, suggesting that the intended changes will no doubt be on a smaller scale than in the 1999 reform. According to the authorities, the reduction in tax receipts in 1999 was close to ½ per cent of GDP.

33. This decision stems from the government's failure to abide by the agreement previously signed with the social partners, which provided for an increase in compensation. Legal precedents suggest, however, that the law (in this case a finance act) takes priority over agreements signed between social partners. As a result, the decision may never be applied.

34. The final decision concerning the award could take some time (2 to 3 years), though the Constitutional Court could intervene to shorten the delay. The decision involves a 2.6 per cent wage catch-up for central government officials, backdated to 1997. On a national accounts basis, any wage increases ought to be charged mainly to the 1997 to 2000 accounts, even if they are awarded in 2002 or 2003. The public debt would also be affected.

35. In view of the historic profile of cyclical disturbances, a deficit of a little less than 1 per cent of GDP would give Spain a 90 per cent confidence margin for staying above the 3 per cent deficit limit over a 3 to 5 year time horizon (Dalsgaard and

De Serres, 1999). A balanced budget thus provides an additional margin for discretionary action of approximately 1 per cent of GDP.

36. In practice, the application of this rule will be adjusted according to the entities concerned. In the case of public corporations, agencies and enterprises, it is designed to promote efficient management so as to ensure that the accounts of the administrative authorities, that oversee these entities, balance.

37. In the case of local governments, the National Local Authorities Commission will have the role of co-ordinator.

38. The European system of national and regional accounts, which will be used, will ensure that the various levels of government are treated uniformly.

39. In particular, they could be imposed if the effect of the Communities' failure to meet the balanced budget objective resulted in Spain infringing the Stability and Growth Pact, and thus having to pay a penalty.

40. If all the fund has not been used up during the year, the remaining amount may not be carried over to the following year but will be used to reduce debt or, in the case of the social security, to increase the reserve fund.

41. The general government deficit since 1980 has averaged 4.1 per cent of GDP, compared with an OECD average of 3.1 per cent.

42. Currently, only seven Communities are directly responsible for managing their health expenditure. However, central government responsibilities in this area should be transferred to the other ten Communities during the current legislature.

43. As drafted, the law does however seem to allow resources to be accumulated in the reserve fund of the social security, to be used when pension expenditure increases.

44. Some countries such as New Zealand, the United Kingdom and Australia have legislated principles rather than rules in order to maintain fiscal discipline. See Atkinson and van den Noord (2001) for a discussion.

45. This employment measure refers to full-time equivalent employment in the national accounts, that is, weighting part-time employment by the time worked. Labour force survey (LFS) employment has grown by even more, averaging more than 4 per cent over the same period. The level of LFS employment is, however, lower than the national accounts measure.

46. Before 2001, collective agreements in some sectors, like construction, already included severance payments for temporary workers.

47. The lack of a well-developed rental market may also explain the lack of labour mobility.

48. The increase in the proportion of temporary work in the public sector reflects employment restrictions implemented since 1996 for all levels of government, that have been overcome by municipalities through fixed-term hiring.

49. In those sectors that had not introduced them through collective agreements.

50. Once the firm recognises that the dismissal is unjustified, it automatically pays higher severance payments, but the dismissal will not be appealed in the courts therefore avoiding bureaucratic costs and the payment of the salary while the process takes place. The 1994 reform attempted to modify this situation, by including "economic" reasons in "justified" dismissals. The 1997 reform went further by specifying more clearly the meaning of those economic reasons; but the situation has barely changed.

51. However, the empirical support for this argument is inconclusive (OECD, 1997).

52. For instance, if a worker has cumulated rights to receive unemployment benefits for one year and is laid off during only one month, he keeps the remaining rights to eleven months of benefits for the next unemployment spell.

53. The EU average rate of accidents is 4 089. In Spain, the highest incidence was in construction (8 008 accidents) and agriculture (6 790).

54. In 1992, at the request of the government, the Tribunal published a comprehensive report on competition that set a number of sectoral priorities for reform. Up to 1995 it published annual competition reports, but not more recently because of a lack of resources. An example of its toughness is the report on the proposed merger of the two largest electricity companies, for which it recommended the imposition of strict conditions on the market share of the new company.

55. The average number of files sent by the Servicio to the Tribunal has increased from 42 per year in the first half of the 90s to 62 in the second half. The number of resolutions of the Tribunal has risen from an average of 82 to 131 over the same period.

56. A ruling of November 1999 by the Constitutional Tribunal allowed for it.

57. Coal production is concentrated in Asturias, an industrial region in the North that suffered heavily from industrial restructuring after the oil shocks of the 70s.

58. Total agricultural support at the EU level in 2000, including direct and price support through import duties and export subsidies, is estimated to have been 38 per cent of total gross farm receipts.

59. Nevertheless, due to the extensive use of agricultural insurance in Spain, the amount of insurance subsidies is higher than the EU average. As a consequence, public expenditure on emergency aid will be lower.

60. These measures are currently being investigated by the EU competition authorities.

61. In practice, as in other European countries, access to the local loop of Telefónica will become operative later, as some of the terms of access have to be negotiated.

62. The three operators are Telefónica Móviles, Airtel and Amena. They have contested the plans of the government to issue new licenses, arguing that they would occupy part of the spectrum awarded to them. Concerning the decision to issue the new licenses, Amena has appealed to the courts.

63. Data from the European Commission show that between 1998 and 2000 the price drops for both residential and business users have been the largest in the European Union.

64. Current costs are those which consider the cost of replacement instead of the historical cost. They are an intermediate step before implementing a model of long-run incremental cost as agreed at the EU level.

65. Resellers of services were allowed to operate in 2000, and four virtual operators will be working from August 2001.

66. The proposed flat rate is for unlimited use during off-peak hours for metropolitan calls to numbers allocated to Internet providers.

67. ADSL and, in general, xDSL technologies use copper cable to transmit data at high speed.

68. In fact, several international providers of ADSL services have entered the Spanish market.

69. Three of them went to the current operators of GSM technologies, and the fourth to a pool of companies under the name of Xfera. Some of the losing candidates have appealed these concessions in the tribunals, although a decision has still to be taken.

70. Not only for mobile telephone companies, but also for local operators through radio access and radio and private TV stations.

71. The original plans of the government were to award these licences during the first quarter of 2001, but the decision has been postponed until next year.

72. The government established a capacity limit of 45 per cent in generation for the merged company, imposed the obligation to sell by auction and declared that compensation for the transition to competition should be reduced.

73. The 1997 reform law concerning the electricity sector limits the share of one single operator in REE to 10 per cent, and the total share of all market participants to 40 per cent.

74. For instance, a contract between *Electricité de France* and REE for 550 megawatts ends only in 2010.

75. The only exception is the regional government of Madrid, which has raised the number of opening Sundays.

76. However, the market share of foreign banks in 1998 was higher than in most other euro area countries (ECB, 2000).

77. Banco Bilbao Vizcaya Argentaria (BBVA) and Banco Santander Central Hispano (BSCH), which controls Banesto.

78. However, some medium-sized banks could follow in the future. For instance, Banco Popular (the third largest commercial bank) has declared itself open to possible agreements with other institutions.

79. The reports from the Competition Tribunal in 1999, prior to the approval of the mergers that created the BBVA and the BSCH, have shown that the level of competition in the sector was high. However, investigations by the EU's competition body on possible agreements among European banks on exchange rate commission fees have involved one large Spanish bank.

80. This is an EU-wide feature. The expected consolidation of the banking industry after the introduction of the single currency has not yet materialised (ECB, 1999).

81. In early 2001 the Bank of Spain was invited to take part in the Supervision Committee of the Bank of International Settlements, partly because of its important supervisory role *vis-à-vis* Spanish banks in Latin America.

82. It is worth noting that Spain was the only country that participated on its own in the multilateral loan to Argentina in December 2000. The Spanish government contributed US$ 1 billion to a total of US$ 39 billion.

83. In 1999, investment in private fixed income assets was equivalent to 13 per cent of GDP, against an average of 44.4 per cent in the euro area and 69.8 per cent in the United States.

84. Between the first quarter of 1999 and the third quarter of 2000 capitalisation increased by 48 per cent (and has reached 70 per cent of GDP so far).

85. The Basque Country and Navarra collect most of their taxes and pay the central government a transfer for central expenses like defence, foreign policy and some infrastructure networks (like airports and ports). The amount they pay is calculated as a percentage of the cost of these services, the weight being the relative value added of each region with respect to the national GDP.

86. For some Autonomous Communities who did not accept the system approved in 1997 and are still ruled by the previous one, the share is 15 per cent, and they are not

allowed to modify rates. They are Andalucía, Extremadura, Castilla-La Mancha and Asturias. Up to now, no regional government has modified the marginal rates of tax, although most have introduced additional deductions, mainly concerning family and housing allowances.

87. This share was a function of several variables (like population, population density, income per capita), although they were fixed at their 1997 level when the personal income tax share was transferred to the regions. The population variables used for establishing regional parameters in 1997 were, however, not updated with the 1996 population census, explaining in part why some regions did not accept the system applied during 1997-2001.

88. In particular, the guarantee schemes would be scrapped, the share of PIT revenues assigned to regions would be raised from 30 to 40 per cent, and part of indirect taxes would also be transferred. Powers to change taxes would be increased for the PIT and introduced for some indirect taxes (alcohol and tobacco).

89. In ten of the Communities expenditure is centrally managed by INSALUD and in the other seven by the Communities themselves.

90. The co-payment is 40 per cent for working persons, nil for retirees and 10 per cent for chronic invalids. Co-payments are capped at ESP 439 in the case of chronic diseases.

91. Assuming that the pharmaceutical consumption of pensioners is 3.3 times higher than that of other persons (as it is for total health spending), their share in total pharmaceutical expenditure should be about 40 per cent.

92. Mark-ups on products costing more than ESP 20 000, which used to be 27.9 per cent for pharmacists and 9.6 per cent for wholesale producers, were capped at ESP 5 580 and ESP 1 384 respectively with effect from August 2000 and were thus reduced for the most expensive products. Pharmacies with sales in excess of ESP 4.6 million per month also had to reduce their margins. The maximum prescribed reduction was 13 per cent for pharmacies with monthly sales in excess of ESP 42 million.

93. In the United States the market share of generic drugs is 40 per cent when measured by volume instead of value.

94. Doctors will receive ESP 125 000 per half-year if they prescribe generic drugs for more than 6 per cent of total prescriptions. These incentives, already introduced in Catalonia, appear to be effective.

95. Hitherto, in the case of expenditure overruns, only the health minister's authorisation was needed for these to be covered. Henceforth, approval by the finance minister is required. If this is given, authorisation will have to be approved by the Council of Ministers and by Parliament.

96. The reference pricing system applies both to working persons and to pensioners. The latter are exempted from co-payment only as to the reference price of the product concerned.

97. In Andalusia the growth of pharmaceutical expenditure over the past eight years amounted to 63.6 per cent, compared with an average of 84.8 per cent for Spain as a whole.

98. This survey, carried out by the private agency Iasist, evaluated the hospitals with six indicators: mortality and risk-adjusted complications, average waiting time, bed occupancy, production cost and transfer to ambulatory services.

99. In the case of cardiac surgery, an emergency plan to reduce the maximum waiting time to 60 days was successfully introduced. The activity of surgical centres has been

increased, the waiting list system standardised and the waiting times for each user clarified. In addition, the options for patients to have their operation in hospitals outside their own region have been expanded.

100. The OECD and the Working group on ageing of the Economic Policy Committee of the European Union have used the Eurostat projections in comparing pension expenditure projections between OECD countries.

101. The dependency ratio – *i.e.* the ratio of persons aged 65 and over to persons aged between 20 and 64, which stood at 27 per cent in 2000 – will only rise by 9½ percentage points until 2025 as against 12½ percentage points for the OECD average. This is because the persons now nearing retirement are the small age groups born during the Spanish civil war.

102. The average retirement age appears to be later than in most European countries, particularly as compared to Italy (59 years) and Finland (60 years).

103. The number of working-age persons should decrease by 0.6 per cent a year between 2000 and 2050, compared with an increase of 0.9 per cent between 1980 and 2000. Since the labour input to production represents about 65 per cent, a reduction of 1.5 percentage points (0.6 – |–0.9|) in growth of that input would cause a fall of 1 percentage point (0.65*1.5) in average potential growth (estimated by the OECD at 2.6 per cent a year on average between 1980 and 2000). If the employment rate does not rise, productivity-induced growth of per capita GDP would be reduced by 18½ per cent owing to the fall in the employment/total population ratio. This estimate of the ageing effect on per capita GDP is close to the European average estimated by Turner *et al.* (1998).

104. A rise in the fertility rate has only a limited effect, since the cohorts of women of childbearing age are becoming progressively smaller. Furthermore, a rise in the rate results in an increase in the working age population only after 20 years.

105. The assumption for increased life expectancy is 4.1 and 2.9 years respectively for men and women over the period from 2000 to 2050 compared with an average of 5.3 and 4.3 years in the other EU countries, a difference of more than one year. On this assumption, the increase in average length of life would be less than one month per year over the next 50 years, as against two to three months per year over the last 35 years.

106. The figures for 1998 somewhat underestimate the size of the foreign population in Spain, since they do not include undocumented immigrants. According to the most recent figures, which incorporate an exceptional legalisation of these immigrants, the foreign population was 940 000 in 2000 or nearly 2½ per cent of the total population, which represents less than half the European average.

107. The criteria for the award of pensions under the non-contributory scheme, created in 1990, are conditions of residence, age, personal/medical situation and resources. To qualify, it is necessary to have resided in Spain for at least ten years (five in cases of disability), of which two consecutively, prior to application for the pension and to be aged over 65, or to be aged between 18 and 65 with more than 65 per cent invalidity.

108. The social security system (INSS, *Instituto Nacional de Seguridad Social*) also has a special fund covering temporary disability. These various schemes, which exist partly for historical reasons, are differentiated by their contribution rates, earnings coverage and by the possibility of access to early retirement, which influence their financial balance.

109. In 2000 the reference income or contribution base was calculated as the average of actual earnings subject to contribution (between an upper and a lower limit) over the

past twelve years. This period will be extended to 15 years as from 2002. The earnings taken into account in this calculation are inflation-indexed for the period prior to the past two years, but earnings in the past two years are not adjusted. The calculation is made on a monthly basis but allows for the fact that pensions are disbursed in the form of 14 monthly payments. In the case of the year 2000, where 12 years are taken into account in computing the reference base, this gives algebraically:

$$RB = [\Sigma\ CB_i + \Sigma(CPI_{25}/CPI_i) * CB_i] / 168$$
$$\quad\ i=1,24 \quad i=25,144$$

where CPI is the consumer price index, CB the contribution base and RB the regulatory base.

110. In 2000 the estimated annual net average wage (net of social security contributions and income tax) was approximately ESP 2.2 million. The gross average wage, with employee contributions added in, was ESP 2.8 million and the maximum pension was ESP 4.3 million.

111. Social security contributions are used essentially to finance pensions, whereas health care expenditure is tax funded (see below). Unemployment insurance contributions are shared between the employee and employer, 1.55 and 6 per cent respectively. Social security contributions are 4.7 per cent for the employee and 23.6 per cent for the employer.

112. This benefit is a differential income supplement that provides a basic income level. The income limit for eligibility for a non-contributory pension is the annual amount of that pension.

113. Out of a total of 8.6 million pensions, 0.7 million received basic income support and nearly 2.5 million were covered by the supplement to the contributory system's minimum pension.

114. In the case of unemployed persons, social security contributions are paid by INEM, the agency that pays out unemployment benefits. However, the contribution base is often reduced to the minimum, particularly when the spell of unemployment is prolonged. This reduces the amount of the pension when unemployment precedes retirement.

115. In 1999, 48.5 per cent of contributory pensions were paid to women. The replacement rate for the widow's pension is 45 per cent in the general scheme and 20 per cent for the orphan's pension.

116. The pension wealth is defined as the net present value of total pensions received by the agent less the total contribution paid. The rate of return is the discount rate that equalises total contributions paid with total benefits received. The higher this rate, the more "profitable" it is to contribute. In the case of the special schemes, the increase in pension due to the rise in the replacement rate these workers receive if they contribute longer does not offset the loss of discounted income they incur because of their additional contributions and their shorter period of pension receipt. In some cases, workers gain nothing by contributing for a longer period since they can receive only the minimum pension.

117. These estimates for Spain are consistent with those obtained by Gil and López-Casasnovas (1999) and Jimeno and Licandro (1999) for the general scheme.

118. According to Boldrin et al., (1999), the rate of return in Spain (amounting to 4 per cent) is higher than in Germany (2.8), France (3.3) and Italy (2.0).

119. In this sense, the special schemes are more generous than the general scheme. This apparent paradox is explained by two major factors: i) the system generates strong incentives to reduce the contribution period (because of the existence of a minimum pension); ii) contribution rates and bases are sometimes capped at a low level in some of these regimes. See Bandrés and Cuenca (1999) for similar results.

120. The pension/pensioner ratio rose from 1.065 to 1.089 between 1988 and 2000. It should be noted that supplements to the minimum pension, on the other hand, are means-tested.

121. Because of this indexation system, pensions rose by 1.6 per cent in real terms between 1996 and 1999.

122. It is difficult, however, to precisely determine the financial situation of the social security system in a historical perspective because of various changes in accounting procedures and the absence of any clear separation of funding sources (Comisiones Obreras, 2000).

123. In the scheme for farm workers the number of contributors per pension was 0.7, compared with 2.7 and 2.8 respectively for the general scheme and the scheme for the self-employed. The standard contribution rate is 28.3 per cent. For farm employees the rate is 11.5 per cent, for self-employed farmers 18.75 per cent and for domestic employees 22 per cent.

124. The rule adopted is that contributions should serve in principle to finance contributory pensions and maternity benefits. State transfers should be used for health care and welfare assistance, family allowances, non-contributory pensions and supplements to the minimum pensions of the contributory system. These latter supplements, which represented 0.7 per cent of GDP in 2000, are still being financed by contributions. The separation of sources of social security finance should be completed in 10 to 12 years.

125. According to Blöndal and Scarpetta (1998), the mean age of retirement of older male workers fell by 6.5 years between 1960 and 1995, one of the steepest falls recorded in the OECD.

126. The retirement rate among men aged 59-63 is two times lower for those with university degrees than for those with no qualifications (Ahn and Mira, 2000). According to this study, the rise in the population's level of education and the arrival at ages 55 to 64 of the small cohorts born between 1937 and 1942 account for 3.3 percentage points of the total rise of 5.9 percentage points in the participation rate for men aged 55-64 over the period 1995-2000. Over the period 2000-20, the population composition effect of the improvement in qualifications should help to increase the participation rate of men aged 55-64 by 4.5 percentage points.

127. Until March 2001 early retirement was only available to those workers who started contributing before January 1967.

128. Since the 1997 reform the replacement rate is 50 per cent from the 15th contribution year. This rate then rises by 3 points a year until the 25th contribution year, then by 2 points a year from the 26th year, reaching and stabilising at 100 per cent from the 35th year.

129. Similar results have been obtained by Boldrin et al. (1997). The high share of persons interrupting their activity before the legal age of retirement might also result from a higher preference for leisure.

130. However, the calculation of implicit tax rates depends on the discount rate used to estimate the present value of the pension wealth. The results shown in the table correspond to a discount rate of 3 per cent. When the discount rate falls, indicating a lower relative value of present time, the implicit tax rate is reduced. For example, with a discount rate of 2 per cent, the implicit tax rate for a person that receives the average wage only becomes positive at age 63 (instead of 62).

131. In 1996, 65 per cent of new pensioners had taken early retirement.

132. The growth in the number of pensions has slowed to around 1 per cent a year since the early 90s, against 6½ per cent between 1980 and 1986. The average age of new invalidity pensioners fell from 51.8 years in 1990 to 50.3 years in 1998.

133. See Blanco (2000). Permanent invalidity pensions are generous as they guarantee a replacement rate of between 75 and 100 per cent for persons aged over 55 and are exempt from income tax.

134. These arrangements may also be financed with entitlements under a firm's private pension plan. Unemployment insurance benefit may extend over a period of three years. In the absence of labour/management agreements or statutory arrangements for aid to workers affected by restructuring, employees aged over 52 may claim an assistance benefit (equivalent to 75 per cent of the minimum wage) until their retirement. However, INEM may refuse to pay this benefit if the income of the person concerned is judged sufficient.

135. In 1999, the number of early retirements stood at just under 49 000, down 40 per cent from 1994. In comparison, there were 83 400 early retirements under the general scheme.

136. There the pension plans are for the most part on a defined-contribution basis, with contributions averaging 6 per cent of the wage, the larger share of which (4.8 per cent on average) is borne by the employer. In sectors like construction, hotels and retailing, where SMEs predominate, arrangements often take the form of a retirement bonus, equal to a few months' pay (García de Quevedo, 1999).

137. The pension plans enjoy great freedom of investment, inasmuch as investments are made *via* organised markets. The annual rate of return of these funds amounted to about 6 per cent in real terms during the past eight years.

138. Since 1995 the number of individual contracts has risen twice as rapidly (25 per cent a year) as that of corporate contracts. Individual investors have been switching from investment funds to pension funds, which enjoy tax relief and offer a comparatively high return.

139. In 1997 only 4.5 per cent of pension plan participants reached the upper limit of contribution. Of the persons with incomes of over ESP 10 million, only 40 per cent reached that limit. From the standpoint of employees, taxation of pension funds, which was reduced between 1997 to 2000, is therefore not an obstacle to the development of private supplementary pension schemes (Plaza and García de Quevedo, 2000).

140. Poverty is most pronounced among the oldest women living alone: 30 per cent of women aged 80-84 live alone, as against only 9 per cent of men in that age group.

141. This question was referred to the Constitutional Tribunal, which has yet to deliver a ruling.

142. According to Alonso and Herce (1998), this "creep" could be more pronounced, and could reach 0.58 percentage point per year between 1996 and 2040. It is also possible

that health costs will increase because, for instance, medical progress will give rise to more costly forms of care, or relative wages of medical practitioners specialising in geriatrics could grow. As the family role diminishes, the need for nursing care will also increase. Conversely, such estimates may overstate the impact of ageing on health expenditure. Older people in fact now remain healthy for longer than they used to, and medical expenditure by those aged over 65 is higher primarily because of the high cost of care during the final months of life (Visco, 2001).

143. The average age at which dependency begins is 72 years. At age 65, life expectancy averages 16.9 years, of which 6.7 years will be disability-free. The average age of people in residential institutions is 85 years (Observatorio de Personas Mayores, 2000).

144. About 10 per cent of the population has supplementary private cover.

145. Medical services in ten of the Autonomous Communities are managed directly by the central administration, through INSALUD, while the remaining seven are directly responsible for such services. These communities receive an allocation from the State budget to cover this expenditure. The process of transferring health service management is expected to be completed during the current legislature.

146. In 1998, there were 112 797 persons receiving at-home care (representing 1.8 per cent of the over-65 population as compared with the 8 per cent called for under the Gerontology Plan); 198 358 places in institutional residences (3.2 per cent of the over-65 population compared with a goal of 3.5 per cent); 60 000 telecare users (0.9 per cent) and 12 134 users of other services (0.15 per cent). In 1998, the coverage rate offered by the various social services for severely dependent persons was estimated at 38 per cent. Waiting lists are growing: the average waiting time for an opening in a public institution is between 1 and 1½ years.

147. These programmes (Gerontology Plan, the Alzheimer's care plan, etc.) are financed through the Institute for Migration and Social Services (IMSERSO). A portion (0.52 per cent) of personal income tax revenues is earmarked for the construction and upgrading of long-term care centres and services.

148. It may also imply that the supervisory authorities are rather more tolerant when it comes to quality standards for private residences in certain cases (Comisiones Obreras, 2000*b*).

149. The demographic projections used for European countries are those of Eurostat (presented above for Spain). As regards the macroeconomic assumptions, annual productivity growth is taken as remaining stable at 1¾ per cent, while unemployment declines progressively to its structural level. In the case of Spain, it drops from 14.2 per cent in 2000 to 4 per cent by 2040. The female participation rate rises in all countries and converges towards 70 per cent in 2050, while the male participation rate remains fairly stable around 80 per cent.

150. The gap between pensions paid and the level of pensions needed to ensure equilibrium between the capitalised value of contributions and the current value of pensions is estimated at 49 per cent of average pensions in 1992, according to Bandrés and Cuenca (1999).

151. Similar results were obtained by Berenguer *et al.* (1999). These estimates of intergenerational transfers are, however, on the high side as they do not take into account the consolidation of the public finances achieved since 1996.

152. Maintaining a primary surplus excluding the pension system induces a sharp fall of indebtedness (by around 70 per cent of GDP) by 2025-30, when the consequences of the ageing process will start to be felt. The strong rise in the public deficit thereafter,

which continues beyond 2050, implies a very marked turnaround with a rapid rise of the public debt.

153. Furthermore, these projections do not take into account the foreseeable increase in the number of early retirements that should derive from the measures adopted in March 2001 (Box 5).

154. The partial inflation-indexing of public service pensions in the scenario prepared by the national experts explains in part the comparatively modest increase in pensions relative to productivity. According to Jimeno (2000), on the other hand, the pensions/productivity ratio could increase from 17 per cent today to more than 30 per cent by 2050.

155. A simple extrapolation of pension expenditure measured as a proportion of GDP until 2050 was also done in a study by the Comisiones Obreras (2000). This shows a much more moderate increase in pension expenditure (1.8 points of GDP between 2025 and 2050) than the other studies. However, this extrapolation is based on the assumption that annual GDP growth remains at 2½ per cent over this period, despite the decline in the working population resulting from the ageing process. On the basis of estimates in the study made by national experts and consolidated by the OECD, output growth could decline from 2.7 per cent between 2000 and 2025 to 0.9 per cent between 2025 and 2050. Using this alternative assumption for economic growth causes pension expenditures to rise by 5.8 percentage points of GDP between 2025 and 2050, an order of magnitude comparable to that found in the other available studies. The assumption that output growth remains at 2½ per cent between 2025 and 2050 would necessarily imply a higher participation rate or a notable acceleration in labour productivity growth from its previous trend, and this in turn would influence the growth of average pensions or their number, a development not allowed for.

156. A higher productivity growth reduces pension spending in proportion to GDP as pensions are solely indexed on price inflation.

157. According to the latest Stability Programme, the public debt should fall by 10 per cent of GDP between 2000 and 2004.

158. The reduction of this possibility of combining widows' pensions with other pensions would however weaken the incentive for women to participate in the labour market.

159. While the development of private occupational plans could help relieve wage pressures, this would not necessarily be the case for labour-cost pressures.

160. A higher employment rate increases temporarily the growth rate of potential output and consequently the financing capacity of the pension regime. Hence a rise in the employment ratio will help to respond to the problems related to the demographic transition as long as its effect is also temporary. However, the increase of employment generates also a pension right and therefore a liability for the pension system. If the system is excessively generous relative to the long-term potential growth of the economy, like in Spain, the pension debt should then rise.

161. The effects of immigration are not necessarily the same for all segments of the population, even if the overall impact of such a policy is probably positive. It must be accompanied, therefore, by measures to compensate potential losers, who generally belong to disadvantaged groups, through policies to promote regional development, urban renewal, education, etc. (Visco, 2000).

Glossary of acronyms

ADSL	Asymmetric Digital Subscriber Line
ALMP	Active Labour Market Policies
BBVA	*Banco Bilbao Vizcaya Argentaria*
BSCH	*Banco Santander Central Hispano*
CMT	*Comisión del Mercado de las Telecomunicaciones* (telecommunications sector regulator)
CNMV	*Comisión Nacional del Mercado de Valores* (stock market supervision authority)
CPI	Consumer Price Index
ECB	European Central Bank
ECOFIN	Economic Policy Committee of the European Union
EPL	Employment Protection Legislation
ESP	Spanish peseta
EU	European Union
GDP	Gross Domestic Product
GSM	Global System for Mobile Communications
GW	Gigawatt
HP	Hodrick-Prescott
ICT	Information and Communication Technology
IMF	International Monetary Fund
INE	*Instituto Nacional de Estadística* (National statistics institute)
INEM	*Instituto Nacional de Empleo* (national agency for employment and unemployment)
INSS	*Instituto Nacional de Seguridad Social* (social security system)
LFS	Labour Force Survey
PAYG	Pay-as-you-go
PHN	*Plan Hidrológico Nacional* (national water plan)
PIT	Personal Income Tax
R&D	Research and Development
REE	*Red Eléctrica Española* (high voltage electricity distribution company)
RIO	Reference Interconnection Offer
SMEs	Small and Medium-sized Enterprises
UMTS	Universal Mobile Telephone Systems (third generation mobile telephone systems)
UN	United Nations

Bibliography

Ahn, N. and P. Mira (1998),
"Job bust, baby bust: the Spanish case", Fundación de Estudios de Economía Aplicada (FEDEA), *Estudios sobre la Economía Española*, EEE12, Madrid, December.

Ahn, N. and P. Mira (2000),
"Labour Force Participation and Retirement of Spanish Older Men: Trends and Prospects", FEDEA, *Documentos de Trabajo*, No. 2000-25, Madrid, December.

Alonso, J. and J.A. Herce (1998),
"El gasto sanitario en España: Evolución reciente y perspectiva", FEDEA, *Textos Express*, No. 98-01, Madrid.

Alonso, J.O., J.L.R. Bara and A.R. Parés (2001),
"Liberalización de mercados e inflación", Fundación de las Cajas de Ahorros Confederadas para la Investigación Económica y Social, *Cuadernos de Información Económica*, No. 160, Madrid, January/February.

Atkinson, P. and P. van den Noord (2001),
"Managing public expenditure: some emerging policy issues and a framework for analysis", OECD, *Economics Department Working Papers*, No. 285.

Balmaseda M., M. Sebastián and P. Tello (2000),
"The Spanish economic 'miracle': a macro perspective", Banco Bilbao Vizcaya Argentaria (BBVA), Research Department, *Situación Spain*, Madrid, June.

Bandrés, E. and A. Cuenca (1999),
"Transfers in Spanish state retirement pensions", *Fiscal Studies*, The Institute for Fiscal Studies, Vol. 20, No. 2, Madrid, pp. 205-219.

BBVA (Banco Bilbao Vizcaya Argentaria) (2000),
Situación Spain, BBVA Research Department, Madrid, October.

BBVA (2001),
"España: cambio en las ponderaciones del IPC", BBVA Resarch Department, *Nota interna*, No. 02/01, Madrid, February.

Bentolila, S. and J.J. Dolado (1994),
"Labour flexibility and wages: lessons from Spain", *Economic Policy*, No. 18, Oxford, Blackwell Publishers.

Berenguer, E., H. Bonin and B. Raffelhüschen (1999),
"Spain: the need for a broader tax base", *Generational Accounting in Europe*, European Economy Reports and Studies, No. 6, Luxembourg, Office for Official Publications of the European Communities.

Blanchard, O. (2001),
"Country adjustments within Euroland. Lessons after two years", *Defining a Macroeconomic*

Framework for the Euro Area. Monitoring the European Central Bank 3, Centre for Economic Policy Research (CEPR), London, March.

Blanco, A. (2000),
"The decision of early retirement in Spain", FEDEA, *Estudios sobre la Economía Española*, EEE76, Madrid.

Blöndal, S. and S. Scarpetta (1998),
"The retirement decision in OECD countries", OECD, *Economics Department Working Papers*, No. 202.

Boldrin, M., J. Dolado, J. Jimeno and F. Peracchi (1999),
"The future of pension systems in Europe. A reappraisal", Paper for the 29th Economic Policy Panel Meeting in Frankfurt, 9-10 April.

Boldrin, M., S. Jiménez-Martín and F. Peracchi (1997),
"Social Security and Retirement in Spain", National Bureau of Economic Research (NBER), *Working Papers*, No. W6136, August.

Bonin, H., J. Gil and C. Patxot (1999),
"Beyond the Toledo agreement: The intergenerational impact of the Spanish pension reform", FEDEA, *Estudios sobre la Economía Española*, EEE38, Madrid, April.

Calmfors, L. and J. Driffil (1988),
"Bargaining Structure, Corporatism and Macroeconomic Performance ", *Economic Policy*, Oxford, Blackwell Publishers, April.

COE (Centre d'observation économique) (2001),
Lettre mensuelle de conjoncture, Chambre de commerce et d'industrie de Paris (CCIP), No. 432, January.

Comisiones Obreras (2000),
El sistema de Seguridad Social español en el año 2000. La renovación del Acuerdo de Pensiones, Confederación sindical de comisiones obreras (CC.OO.), Cuadernos de Información Sindical No. 2, Madrid, October.

Comisiones Obreras (2000b),
Los servicios de atención a las personas dependientes (Propuesta de inclusión en la renovación del Acuerdo de Pensiones), Confederación sindical de CC.OO., Cuadernos de Información Sindical No. 10, Madrid, December.

Consejo Económico y Social (CES) (2000),
"Vida laboral y prejubilaciones", *Colección Informes*, No. 2/2000, Madrid.

Dalsgaard, T. and A. De Serres (1999),
"Estimating prudent budgetary margins for 11 EU countries: a simulated SVAR model approach", OECD, *Economics Department Working Papers*, No. 216.

ECB (European Central Bank) (1999),
Monthly Bulletin, Frankfurt, April.

ECB (2000),
Monthly Bulletin, Frankfurt, April.

Economic Policy Committee (2000),
"Progress report to the Ecofin Council on the impact of population ageing on public pension systems", European Commission, EPC/ECFIN581/00-EN REV1, Brussels, 6 November.

European Commission (2000),
Eighth Survey on State Aid in the European Union, Brussels, April.

European Commission (2001),
   European Economy, Economic Trends, Supplement A, March/April No. 3/4.

Flaquer, L.(2000),
   "Las políticas familiares en una perspectiva comparada", Fundación "la Caixa".

Fundación Cotec para la Innovación Tecnológica (2000),
   La innovación en las tecnologías de la informacion y las telecomunicaciones, Informes Cotec.

García de Quevedo, J. (1999),
   "El ahorro privado en previsión social", *Boletín económico de* ICE (Información Comercial
   Española), Ministerio de Economía y Hacienda, No. 2619, Madrid, June.

García de Quevedo, J. (1999*b*),
   "Instrumentación de los compromisos por pensiones de las empresas españolas. Situación actual y perspectivas", *Boletín económico de* ICE, Ministerio de Economía y Hacienda, No. 2606, Madrid, February.

Gil, J. and G. López-Casasnovas (1999),
   "Redistribution in the Spanish pension system: An approach to its life time effects",
   FEDEA, *Estudios sobre la Economía Española*, EEE55, Madrid.

Hauser, R. (1999),
   "Adequacy and Poverty Among Retired People", *International Social Security Review*, International Social Security Association, Vol. 52, No. 3/99, Oxford, Blackwell.

Herce, J. and J. Alonso (1998),
   "Los efectos económicos de la Ley de consolidación de la Seguridad Social. Perspectivas financieras del sistema de pensiones tras su entrada en vigor", FEDEA, *Documentos
   de Trabajo* 98-16, September.

Herce, J.A. (2001),
   "La privatización de las pensiones en España", FEDEA, *Documentos de Trabajo*, No. 2001-01,
   Madrid.

Herce, J.A. and J. Alonso-Meseguer (2000),
   "La reforma de las pensiones ante la revisión del Pacto de Toledo", La Caixa, Sevicio
   de Estudios, *Colección Estudios Económicos*, No. 19, Barcelona.

IMSERSO (Instituto de Migraciones y de Servicios Sociales) (1999),
   Memoria 1999, Ministerio de Trabajo y Asuntos Sociales, Madrid.

INE (Instituto Nacional de Estadística) (2000),
   Encuesta sobre la Discapacidades, Deficiencias y Estado de Salud, 1999, Madrid.

INSALUD (1999),
   Programa de atención a las personas mayores, Instituto Nacional de la Salud, Madrid.

Jimeno, J. (2000),
   "El Sistema de Pensiones Contributivas en España: Cuestiones básicas y perspectivas
   en el medio plazo", FEDEA, *Documentos de Trabajo*, No. 2000-15, Madrid.

Jimeno, J. and O. Licandro (1999),
   "La tasa interna de rentabilidad y el equilibrio financiero del sistema español de pen-
   siones de jubilación", *Investigaciones Económicas*, Vol. XXIII(1), Fundación Empresa
   Pública, Madrid, pp. 129-143.

La Caixa (2000),
   The Spanish Economy: Monthly Report, No. 228, Caja de Ahorros y pensiones de Barcelona,
   September.

Leahy, M., S. Schich, G. Wehinger, F. Pelgrin and T. Thorgeirsson (2001),
   "Contributions of financial systems to growth in OECD countries", OECD, *Economics Department Working Papers*, No. 280.

Ministerio de Trabajo y Asuntos Sociales (1996),
   La Seguridad Social en el umbral del siglo XXI, Colleción Seguridad Social, No. 14, Madrid.

Ministerio de Trabajo y Asuntos Sociales (2000),
   Informe Económico Financiero a los Presupuestos de la Seguridad Social, Año 2000, Madrid.

Observatorio de Personas Mayores (2000),
   Las personas mayores en España: Informe 2000, IMERSO, Ministerio de Trabajo y Asuntos Sociales, Vol. I, Madrid.

OECD (1994),
   The OECD Jobs Study, Paris.

OECD (1997),
   "Economic performance and the structure of collective bargaining", OECD *Employment Outlook*, Paris.

OECD (1998),
   Maintaining Prosperity in an Ageing Society, Paris.

OECD (1998b),
   OECD *Economic Surveys: Spain*, Paris.

OECD (1999),
   Implementing the OECD *Jobs Strategy: Assessing Performance and Policy*, Paris.

OECD (2000),
   "Revised OECD measures of structural unemployment", OECD *Economic Outlook*, No. 68, Paris, December.

OECD (2000b),
   Science, Technology and Industry Outlook, Paris.

OECD (2000c),
   Regulatory Reform in Spain, OECD Reviews of Regulatory Reform, Paris.

OECD (2000d),
   OECD *Economic Surveys: Spain*, Paris.

OECD (2000e),
   "Eligibility criteria for unemployment benefits", OECD *Employment Outlook*, Paris.

OECD (2000f),
   The Price of Water: Trends in OECD Countries, Paris.

OECD (2001),
   "Fiscal implications of ageing: projections of age-related spending", OECD *Economic Outlook*, No. 69, Paris, June.

Ortega Díaz, M.I. (1999),
   "Las bolsas españolas: una análisis económico", Fundación de las Cajas de Ahorros Confederadas para la Investigación Económica y Social, *Perspectivas del Sistema Financiero*, No. 65, Madrid.

Plaza, J.R. and J. García de Quevedo (2000),
   "Apuntes sobre el funcionamiento del sistema de planes de pensiones", *Boletín económico de* ICE, Ministerio de Economía y Hacienda, No. 2659, July.

Samuelson, P. (1958),
"An Exact Consumption-Loan Model of Interest with or without the Social Contrivance of Money", *The Journal of Political Economy*, Vol. 66, No. 6, The University of Chicago Press.

Turner, D., C. Giorno, A. de Serres, A. Vourc'h and P. Richardson (1998),
"The macroeconomic implications of ageing in a global context", OECD, *Economics Department Working Papers*, No. 193.

UGT (Unión General de Trabajadores) (1999),
"La protección de las personas dependientes y su vinculación con la creación de empleo", *Gabinete Técnico Confederal* UGT, Madrid.

Visco, I. (2000),
"Immigration, development and the labour market", paper presented at an international conference: "Migration: Scenarios for the 21st Century", Rome, 12-14 July.

Visco, I. (2001),
"Paying for pensions: how important is economic growth?", paper presented at the CSIS conference: "Managing the Global Ageing Transition. A Policy Summit of the Global Ageing Initiative", Zurich, 22-24 January.

Annex I

Changes to the method of calculating the consumer price index

The method of calculating the consumer price index (CPI) was modified at the start of 2001 and will undergo further changes in January 2002. These changes are part of the process of harmonising the price indices of the EU countries. The aim is to compile an index with a weighting that is updated regularly, whereas at present the weighting is fixed and based on the 1991-92 household survey. This will allow to take better account of changes in products and in their quality, and in the structure of consumers' expenditure. Since 1997, the National Statistical Institute (INE) has been drawing up a quarterly survey of households' budgets which will be used to adjust, on an ongoing basis, the relative weights of the various groups of goods and services in the index, and to include new products in order to keep it representative.

The modifications to the CPI at the start of 2001 consist of three main changes:

- A change in the classification of the groups of products in the price index, which now has 12 categories instead of 8 previously.
- Re-weighting of the various groups of products: the weight of food and clothes was reduced while that of housing, transport, telecommunications, hotels and cafes was increased.
- A change in the way tariffs are counted in the index, actual expenditure now being taken into account. Thus, in the case of telecommunications, it is the average telephone bill and no longer the number of calls that is taken into account to estimate the price changes.

There exists no official estimate of the impact of these changes, which were implemented in January 2001. According to BBVA (2001), the rise in the price index in 2000 would have been 0.1 to 0.2 percentage point higher if it had been computed with the new method.

The second set of modifications scheduled for 2002 will involve bigger changes in the way the CPI is compiled:

- The weighting of the various components of the CPI will be updated annually so that new products are taken into account regularly.
- Sales and price reductions will be taken into account, which will increase the seasonality of the series (in January and August).
- A more thorough re-basing of the index will be carried out every five years, with updating of the sample and including methodological improvements.
- Quality effects will be taken into account by trying to use a hedonic regression method jointly with improvements to the *ad hoc* methods used currently. This should primarily affect the non-energy industrial goods component (one third of the index).
- The number of establishments and prices surveyed will be increased.

Annex II

The liberalisation package of June 2000

In June 2000 the government published a Royal Decree that includes reforms of several sectors, mostly affecting product markets. The package included, among others, the following measures:

Competition policy

- Mergers will not go into effect until they are approved by the government.
- The same shareholder cannot participate on the board of more than one company in the following sectors: electricity, gas, oil distribution, fixed and mobile telephony. In cases when a shareholder has a stake of more than 3 per cent in more than one company in the same sector, the person will not be allowed to exercise their voting rights for more than 3 per cent in more than one firm. Regulatory bodies may allow for exceptions to this rule.

Telecommunications

- The dominant operator, *Telefónica*, was obliged to publish its cost accounts, which has helped to determine tariffs to the local loop, to finish the tariff re-balancing of Telefónica, and to control that prices charged by the incumbent are cost-oriented.
- The local loop was opened to competition in January 2001.
- The dominant operator introduced carrier pre-selection for local calls as from November 2000.
- A lump-sum Internet rate at non-peak hours was set at ESP 2 750 per month.
- A lump-sum rate for local calls has been established.

Electricity

- Any company with a share in the generation market larger than 40 per cent will not be able to expand its capacity in the next five years (which affects *Endesa*), while if the share is between 20 and 40 per cent the period will be of three years (*Iberdrola*). This ban does not apply to the plants already under construction (a total capacity 30 GW for the sector, when the actual capacity is 55 GW).
- The full liberalisation of the market has been brought forward to 2003 (instead of 2007). By that date all consumers will be able to choose the provider. Large consumers have been allowed to do so since July 2000.

- The reduction of regulated electricity prices for small consumers for the next three years will be at most 9 per cent.
- Other measures: introduction of futures contracts in the wholesale market; phasing out of tariffs for high voltage consumers by 2007; access of large consumers to the transmission and distribution networks at lower prices.

Natural gas

- Full liberalisation has been brought forward from 2008 to January 2003. By that date all consumers will be able to choose their provider.
- From January 2003, the maximum market share of a single company in distribution will be 70 per cent.
- The end of the moratorium on building new distribution networks for companies other than *Gas Natural* has been brought forward from 2008 to 2005.
- The capital of E*nagás*, the wholesale distributor, which is currently owned by Gas Natural, the incumbent operator, will be opened to competitors. The maximum share that can be owned by a single operator will be 35 per cent. The cost of access to the wholesale network has been reduced by 8 per cent.
- Gas Natural will sell 25 per cent of its contract with the main foreign supplier (the Algerian company *Sonatrach*) to competitors. This is a temporary measure that applies until 2004, allowing other operators to negotiate their own contracts in the meantime.

Oil distribution

- Any company with a distribution share over 30 per cent (15 per cent) will not be able to expand its distribution capacity over the next 5 years (3 years).
- At least one petrol station will be authorised in every hypermarket. The petrol station will not be allowed to sign an exclusivity contract with refiners.
- The capital of CLH, which operates the network pipeline and storage facilities, will be opened to competitors (it is currently owned by the three large refiners). No single company will be allowed to own more than 25 per cent. The maximum combined stake or voting rights for all Spanish refining companies will be 45 per cent.
- Periodically owners of petrol stations will send price information to the Ministry of Economy, which will publish it.
- There will be a minimum number of petrol stations in every seaport.

Road transport

- The time period for concessions in regular passenger transport has been reduced from a period of 8-20 years to 6-15 years.

Land

- In order to limit the discretion of municipalities in regulating land development, they will have to justify the refusal of land development plans. Development can start if no refusal is received within six months.
- Real estate brokerage is no longer reserved for a specific professional group.

Retail distribution

- All retail shops will be allowed to open at least 90 hours per week, and 12 Sundays per year. Regional governments may extend these limits. Previously the limits were 72 hours per week, and 8 Sundays per year.
- Business hours for small and medium-sized stores (up to 300 square metres of surface) have been completely liberalised, subject to a maximum limit established by regional governments.

Pharmacies

- Pharmacies are able to make discounts of up to 10 per cent on certain drugs.
- Margins are fixed from a certain price onwards, and they are widened for generics (from 27.9 to 33 per cent).

Other measures

- In professional services, notaries have been allowed to make discounts of up to 10 per cent, and free tariffs are established for large operations (above ESP 1 billion). Regulated tariffs for property registrars and real estate development transactions have been established.
- Banks have been required to inform customers that they may choose their own notary and insurance company when arranging a mortgage.

Annex III
Recent labour market reform measures

In March 2001 the government approved a deepening of the 1997 labour market reform. The measures adopted include:

- An extension of the new permanent contract introduced in the 1997 labour market reform beyond May 2001. The contract carries firing costs of 20 days of wages per year of work, for "justified" dismissals, and 33 days of wages per year worked, for "unjustified" dismissals.

- The permanent contract with reduced firing costs will continue to apply to specific groups (workers aged 18-29, workers with a temporary contract, workers aged over 45, workers that have been unemployed for more than one year, women in some professions), and has been extended to young workers (now defined as those aged between 16 and 30), long-term unemployed (for more than 6 months), unemployed women in sectors where they are underrepresented (most of them) and disabled workers.

- Temporary contracts will be penalised with firing costs of 8 days of wages per year of work (previously there were firing costs in some sectors, established in collective agreements).

- New rules for part-time employment: the definition of part-time work raises the working time from 77 per cent of normal hours to 99 per cent. "Complementary" hours (those beyond the normal working time, but paid at the same wage as normal hours), which can amount to up to 25 per cent of normal hours, will be freely distributed within a year. Previously, they could only be distributed within a quarter, thus restraining the cumulation of hours in those periods of the year with higher demand.

- Temporary subsidies to social security contributions continue to support the creation of permanent employment: between 45 and 60 per cent of social charges for workers aged over 45, between 25 and 70 per cent for women, and between 20 and 60 per cent for the long term unemployed.

- Other measures include: the suppression of social security contributions for women for two years after giving birth; the ability for new immigrants and for the socially excluded (those who have been unemployed for more than three years) to use special "training" and "inclusive" contracts (*contratos de formación* and *contrato de inserción*), which also have lower firing costs and subsidies to social charges.

Annex IV

Uncertainties regarding the demographic projections

Several sets of long-term demographic projections, including those of Eurostat, the United Nations (UN), the National Institute of Statistics, (Instituto Nacional de Estadística, INE) and Fernández-Cordón (Herce et Alonso Meseguer, 2000), are available for Spain.[1] These projections give similar indications concerning the ageing process (Table A1): they all point to a moderate ageing process until 2020 followed by a steep rise in the dependency ratio and a decline in the population thereafter. The magnitude of these trends depends, however, on the assumptions used with respect to the fertility rate, life expectancy and immigration:

– According to Eurostat and Fernández-Cordón, the fertility rate will rise from 1.2 to 1.5 between 2000 and 2020-25, then stabilise at 1.5 until 2050. The INE scenario is based on a slightly weaker rise of the fertility rate (from 1.2 to 1.4) between 2000 and 2020. According to the United Nations, the fertility rate will reach 1.7 in 2050, but with a slower initial pick-up than in the other projections since it will be only 1.3 in 2020.

– According to Eurostat, life expectancy at birth will increase by 4.1 years (from 74.9 to 79 years) for males and by 2.9 years (from 82.1 to 85 years) for females between 2000 and 2050. INE projections are based on similar assumptions to those of Eurostat.[2] The UN projections assume slightly larger increases in lifetimes (0.5 to 0.7 year more) and the Fernández-Cordón projections slightly smaller ones (0.5 year less).

– According to Eurostat, net immigration will increase from 30 000 persons a year at present to 60 000 persons a year from 2010. The INE projection is based on stable immigration of 130 000 persons a year over the next 50 years which prolongs the large net inflow of immigrants recorded in recent years. On the other hand, the Fernández-

Table A1. **Demographic projections**

	Rise in the old-age dependency ratio 27.1 per cent in 2000, percentage points				Growth of working-age population Per cent			
	INE	Eurostat	UN	Cordón	INE	Eurostat	UN	Cordón
2000-20	6.8	6.0	6.6	6.9	2.0	−0.6	−5.1	−2.6
2020-50	28.1	32.5	44.4	33.4	−21.9	−27.0	−39.1	−29.2
2000-50	34.9	38.5	51.0	40.3	−20.3	−27.4	−42.2	−31.1

Source: Eurostat, United Nations, Herce and Alonso Meseguer (2000) and information provided by INE.

Cordón projections assume stable immigration at 30 000 per year, whereas the UN projections assume zero immigration from 2015.

The sensitivity of these projections to changed assumptions for fertility rate, life expectancy and immigration is fairly limited. Simulations made by Eurostat show that:

- A 0.2 point rise in the fertility rate (from 1.5 to 1.7) brings about a 6 per cent increase in the working age population by 2050 relative to the baseline scenario. The induced reduction of the old age dependency ratio amounts to 3 to 4 percentage points by 2050.

- A net immigration increase of some 30 000 persons a year reduces the dependency ratio by 3 to 4 percentage points and increases the working-age population by 6 to 7 percentage points by 2050 relative to the baseline scenario. Given the prospect of a rise of more than 38 percentage points in the dependency ratio between 2000 and 2050, holding the ratio at its initial level would necessitate a massive intake of immigrants, over ten times more than that recorded in the 1990s, which is unrealistic.

- An increase of two years in life expectancy by 2050 raises the dependency ratio by 5 percentage points at that horizon and has a negligible effect on the working-age population.

Notes

1. These demographic projections extend up to 2050. In the case of the INE, the projections are being currently revised and will be published at the end of June 2001.

2. However, life expectancy for females until 2020 is expected to be significantly larger in the INE scenario than in the UN and other projections, with an increase by close to 3 years between 2000 and 2020 against around 2 years in the other cases.

Annex V

The Toledo Pact: measures to improve the public pension system and their impact

Following the deterioration of social security finances as a result of the 1993 recession, a process of parliamentary deliberation on the future of social security was initiated, culminating in the ratification of the Toledo Pact by Congress in 1995. Further to that pact, the government and social partners signed an agreement that served as a basis for the legislation passed in 1997 to consolidate and rationalise the social security system. This reform introduced several measures to improve the long-term financial sustainability of the retirement pension system, make it more equitable and clarify its financing arrangements.

The most important measure was the progressive raising from 8 to 15 years by 2002 of the number of contribution years that determine the reference income in the calculation of pensions (in 1985 the number of years had already been increased from two to eight). According to the OECD's estimates, this change had the effect of lowering pensions by about 3 per cent from their pre-reform level. Another measure taken was to align the contribution ceilings for the different occupational categories in the general scheme with the ceiling for the highest category. This measure has increased the system's resources but pension entitlements as well. The earnings replacement rate used in calculating the pensions of persons with less than 25 contribution years was lowered in order to encourage workers to contribute longer. In addition, the indexation of pensions to the consumer price index was guaranteed by law. Finally, it was decided to tighten the checks on benefits for persons with permanent disability.

These measures were offset by changes designed to make the system more equitable. They included an upward adjustment of widows' pensions, a broader eligibility of orphans' pension entitlements and increased entitlements for early retirees having contributed for more than 40 years (through a lowering of the pension-reduction coefficient from 8 to 7 per cent for each year of pre-retirement). Finally, the reform has facilitated pension eligibility for persons in non-standard employment. Thus eligibility for persons working part-time was improved in 1999, which should encourage the development of this type of employment.

As regards social security financing, the separation of funding sources was written into the law. Insurance benefits have to be financed by contributions and assistance benefits by tax. The law also provided for the creation of a reserve fund to retain social security surpluses.

Overall, the 1997 reform had very little impact on pension expenditure: the measures to increase revenues or reduce spending were offset by those that increased expenditure (Herce and Alonso, 1998 and Bonin *et al.*, 1999). And some of the Toledo Pact's recommendations, such as rationalisation of the special schemes and their integration into the general scheme were not implemented. However, the law now requires a regular review of the financial situation of the pension schemes and that has improved the understanding by the social partners and alerted public opinion to the consequences of population ageing.

Annex VI

Internal rate of return of the public pension system

The purpose of this annex is to clarify the conditions for equilibrium of pay-as-you-go pension schemes, with the aid of a model borrowed from Samuelson (1958), to provide details concerning the assumptions used in calculating the internal rates of return mentioned in the main text, and to indicate the sensitivity of the findings to the choice of assumptions.[1]

Condition for equilibrium of a PAYG pension system

The condition for financial equilibrium of a PAYG system can be derived simply in the case of an economy in which individuals live two periods and two generations coexist: workers and retirees.

In this economy, where N_t denotes the population, e_t the employment rate, w_t the average wage and τ the rate of contribution serving to finance pensions, the receipts of the pension system at period of retirement will be equal to $\tau * (w_t * e_t * N_t)$. If the individuals living at t-1 have probability σ of being still alive at t and drawing a pension with a replacement rate of α, pension expenditure will be equal to the product of the number of retirees ($\sigma\, e_{t-1}\, N_{t-1}$) multiplied by the average amount of the pension ($\alpha\, w_{t-1}$). The balance B_t of the pension system at t will then be equal to:

$$B_t = \tau * (w_t * e_t * N_t) - \alpha * \sigma * (w_{t-1} * e_{t-1} * N_{t-1}) \tag{1}$$

For the system to be in surplus, it is necessary that $B_t > 0$, that is to say:

$$(e_t N_{t-1} / e_{t-1} N_{t-1}) * (w_t / w_{t-1}) > (\alpha * \sigma / \tau) \tag{2}$$

The first term of the inequality [2] represents the rise in the pension system's receipts, which is calculated as the product of employment growth multiplied by wage growth. In the case of a steady-state economy where real wage growth is equal to productivity growth, this term corresponds to output growth.

The second term is equal to the return that the pension system offers to contributors. Individuals who contribute $\tau * w_{t-1}$ in the first period of their life will obtain, with survival probability σ, the pension $\alpha * w_{t-1}$. The rate of return on their contributions is therefore: $1 + r = (\alpha * \sigma / \tau)$.

If employment growth is denoted by n and productivity growth by ω, the formula [2] indicates that on an equilibrium growth path a PAYG system, to be in surplus, must offer its contributors a return lower than the rate of output growth.

$$(1 + n) * (1 + \omega) > (1 + r) \tag{3}$$

Calculation of the internal rate of return for categories of individuals

The internal rate of return that contributors receive from the pension system can be calculated for several categories of individuals defined according to their earnings record, life expectancy and the parameters of the pension system. This is the discount rate r, which equalises the present values of contributions paid in and benefits paid out, as in the following equation:

$$\tau * \Sigma w_t / (1 + r)^{t-1} = \Sigma p_t / (1 + r)^{t-1} \qquad [4]$$
$$ _{t=1...S} _{t=S+1...K}$$

where K represents the period of the individual's entire lifetime, S the period of his working life and p_t the amount of his pension at period t.

In an approach similar to the one used by Jimeno and Licandro (1999) and presented in the main text, *theoretical* internal rates of return for the different pension schemes and several categories of individuals have been estimated on the basis of various parameters of the pension system for the purpose of defining the amounts of old-age pensions p_t.[2] These rates of return do not take account of the historical trend of pension contribution rates, nor do they incorporate detailed information on the actual careers of contributors. However, Gil and López-Casasnovas (1999) have worked along those lines in order to compare the trends over time in rates of return for different cohorts. Their findings were that the older cohorts (1935, 1945) have received higher internal rates of return on their contributions than the younger cohorts (1955, 1965).[3]

Sensitivity of estimates to the system's parameters

Estimates of the internal rate of return of the pension system depend on three factors: demographic (life expectancy), economic (productivity growth, income level) and regulatory. Most of the parameters concerning the last factor derive directly from the rules governing the pension system. These define the method of calculating pensions, *i.e.* the reference income and the replacement rate, but also the contribution rates and bases. The contribution rate, which for example is set at 28.3 per cent in the general regime, is used to finance all the benefits paid out by the contributory system, which include not only old-age pensions but also invalidity pensions, widow's and orphan's pensions and maternity benefits. In the absence of a specific rate assigned to the financing of old-age pensions, it is therefore necessary to estimate the share of contributions financing this type of benefit in order to calculate the system's rate of return. As in the other studies available on this subject, the proportion of contributions that go to finance old-age pensions has been estimated as a function of the overall contribution rate and of the ratio of old-age pension expenditure to total contributory pension expenditure (67.6 per cent in 1999). For the general regime, it was accordingly estimated that the rate of contribution assigned to old-age pension financing was 19.1 (= 28.3*0.676) per cent. An increase of 1 percentage point in this contribution rate lowers the internal rate of return of the scheme by 0.18 point.

Table 21 in the main text shows the sensitivity of estimates of the rate of return of the general scheme to economic and demographic parameters. The tests carried out show that the rate varies between 3½ and 4½ per cent depending on the assumptions. More specifically:

– The rate of return increases when life expectancy rises since people collect their pension longer. An extra year of life expectancy between 77 and 81 causes the rate of return to rise by 0.18 percentage point on average.[4] If this increase concerns the population average, Samuelson's equilibrium condition implies that an equivalent permanent increase in potential production growth is needed to maintain the pension scheme in equilibrium. If there is no permanent increase in labour supply, labour efficiency has to increase.

– If trend labour productivity (and real wages) increase, the internal rate of return of the system rises too.[5] However, the method of calculating pensions and the system of indexation on prices implies that an increase of one percentage point in labour efficiency causes the internal rate of return to rise by only half that amount (0.48 point). Efficiency gains thus have a positive but limited impact on the financial situation of the system. In the case of the previous example, an increase of one year in average life expectancy requires for example an increase of 0.36 percentage point in the growth of trend labour efficiency for the system to remain viable.

Samuelson's condition of equilibrium between average growth of potential production and the internal rate of return depends on the time frame adopted. Between 2000 and 2050, on the assumption of an annual rise in trend factor productivity of 1¾ per cent, the potential growth of the economy is estimated at 1¾ per cent per year in the projections prepared by national experts and co-ordinated by the OECD. However, this average masks a sharp decrease from 2025. Between 2000 and 2025, potential growth could average 2¾ per cent a year but would be less than 1 per cent between 2025 and 2050. It is thus from 2025 that the problems of the financial viability of the system would become particularly acute. However, a comparison of the rate of return (about 4 per cent) and potential growth between 2000 and 2025 suggests that the system would also start to come under strain during this period, and thus earlier than the projections prepared by national experts indicate. This would be particularly so if average pensions continue to rise more rapidly than real wages, as has been the case during the past 20 years. However, this assumption is not adopted by these projections, which assume that pensions will grow slightly less rapidly than real wages (and productivity) between 2000 and 2025 (Table 26). There is thus a risk that this scenario underestimates the consequences of the system's generosity on the increase in average pensions and, by the same token, the total growth of pension expenditure in coming years.

Notes

1. This annex repeats the approach used by Jimeno and Licandro (1999) and also Gil and López-Casasnovas (1999) and Boldrin *et al.* (1999).

2. The parameters used in these estimates are those applying in 2000 (or from 2002 to take account of the extension to 15 years of the period of earnings serving to determine the reference income used in computing pensions). The calculations are based on annual and not monthly data, which constitutes a slight simplification relative to the system's actual functioning.

3. The rise in contributions for the younger generations has more than offset the increase in their length of life. Contribution bases in the 60s and 70s were well below real wages.

4. Thus, for an equivalent income and career, women have a higher internal rate of return than men. In contrast, the internal rate of return of this scheme hardly varies according to the level of income since the existence of a minimum and maximum pension is coupled with a floor and ceiling on contributions.

5. Thus, the system can be regressive for persons with a salary between the maximum and minimum contributions due to the fact that pensions are calculated on the basis of the final years of income and not on a person's entire working career (Gil and López-Casasnovas, 1999).

Annex VII

Corporate supplementary pension systems: pension funds and insurance contracts

Corporate pension schemes rest on different types of arrangements and financial instruments: pension funds, group insurance contracts, mutual insurance and companies' internal funds. In accordance with a European directive, a process of externalisation of these pension schemes has begun and the relevant financial liabilities should be removed from corporate balance sheets by 16 November 2002.* The fact that the corporate schemes will be managed by external financial establishments will make it possible to guarantee the pension agreements in the event of business failure. Ultimately, corporate schemes will rest on only two types of financial instrument: group insurance contracts and occupational pension funds, which differ as to tax treatment and employee's entitlements. Pension agreements based on insurance contracts allow employers considerable oversight of the funds invested in the relevant insurance schemes, whereas those based on pension funds guarantee an employee's entitlement to a supplementary pension even if they leave their employer. These changes should make private corporate pension plans more attractive to employees.

Private pension funds and insurance contracts present distinctly different features with respect to tax treatment and employees' rights.

Employees' pension rights

- The supplementary benefit agreements of pension funds constitute entitlements awarded irreversibly to employees, who retain them even if they leave their employer. These pension plans, which are negotiated in the context of collective bargaining, must apply to all employees.

- Insurance contracts, unlike pension funds, may be confined to certain employees. They do not necessarily confer a definite pension right, but only a promise of entitlement in cases where the employer does not credit the insurance premium to the workers. In such cases the employee is not the holder of the funds invested and loses his pension rights if he leaves a firm.

Tax treatment

- As regards the tax treatment of employees, private supplementary pension agreements based on pension funds benefit from deferred taxation since they represent

---

* Financial enterprises are entitled, under certain conditions, to continue to have their pension funds managed internally. After the cut-off date, non-compliant firms will have to pay a fine of between ESP 5 million and ESP 15 million. Firms will have 10 to 15 years to ensure that their schemes are fully funded.

deferred income. Contributions to these funds (employee and employer) can be deducted from the income tax base. Contributions are tax-deductible up to ESP 1.2 million a year or 25 per cent of earnings (whichever amount is lower). The deduction, which is increased by ESP 0.3 million a year if the spouse does not work or has a yearly income of less than ESP 1.2 million, is larger for persons aged over 52. It reaches a maximum of ESP 2.5 million or 40 per cent of earnings for persons aged 65 and for the disabled. Benefits from these pension plans are paid in the form of an annuity and taxed as earned income. If a lump sum payment is made, the rate of tax varies according to the length of time the plan has been held. Lump sum payments benefit from a tax-exemption of between 40 and 75 per cent depending on the number of years that the plan has been held.

– In the case of insurance-based pension systems, participants have to pay tax only when they have a firm pension right, *i.e.* when the employer credits the insurance premium to them. Unlike the case with pension funds, taxation is not deferred and the premium credited is taxed as earned income. Benefit payments under the insurance contract are subject to ordinary income tax. Only the difference between the contribution and the accumulated saving is taxed, and a 40 per cent deduction applies if the benefit is paid out as an annuity.

– Use of the pension fund system allows the employer to deduct his contribution from the corporation tax base. The amounts paid in are exempt from social security contributions. In the case of insurance-based plans, the employer can deduct the premium from the corporation tax base only when it is credited to the employee, who then becomes the holder of the pension rights. If the premium is not credited, the employer retains the rights and cannot deduct the premium from his tax base until benefits are paid.

Annex VIII

Calendar of main economic events

2000

February

A new law that regulates immigrants' rights (*Ley de* Extranjería) enters into force.

An alliance between BBVA and Telefónica is formed to exchange capital and collaborate on projects such as Internet banking and a mobile telephone payments system.

March

Four licences of third generation mobile telephony (UMTS) are awarded to the three existing operators of GSM telephones and to Xfera.

The ruling party (*Partido Popular*) wins the general elections, obtaining an absolute majority.

The National Employment Plan for 2000 is presented to Parliament.

April

The government approves the updated version of the Stability Programme 1999-2003 that aims at a general government surplus of 0.3 per cent of GDP by 2003.

June

The government presents a liberalisation package that includes measures on a large number of sectors, including telecommunications, electricity, natural gas, oil distribution and retailing (a full account of measures taken is provided in Annex II).

September

The national water plan (*Plan hidrológico nacional*) is presented to Parliament. It includes large investments in water projects throughout the country and a project to canalise water from the Ebro river to the east and south east of the country.

October

The two largest electricity companies, Endesa and Iberdrola, announce their merger.

After demonstrations against petrol price rises, the government approves various measures to help the sectors concerned (road transport, agriculture, fishing, taxi drivers) that amount to ESP 120 billion (1.2 per cent of GDP).

The draft budget for 2001 is presented to Parliament for approval. The budget is based on a growth assumption of 3.6 per cent, and targets a zero deficit for the general government. Main measures include the maintenance of hiring restrictions for civil servants, a wage increase of 2 per cent (in line with the official inflation projection of the government) and a freeze of excise taxes on alcohol, tobacco and fuels. Expenditure priorities are infrastructure and R&D.

The government launches a draft budget stability law that aims to impose a balanced budget on all levels of government unless exceptional circumstances occur.

December

The law accompanying the budget incorporates some additional measures: like a new tax on the electro-magnetic spectrum used (among others) by mobile telephones, the suppression of taxes when switching mortgage loans between banks and subsidies to large families that buy cars.

2001

January

Fixed telephony is fully liberalised with the unbundling of the access to *Telefónica*'s network.

The High Court rules that civil servants' wage increases for 1996 agreed between trade unions and the previous government, and subsequently overruled by the 1997 Budget, have to be paid. The government appeals the decision to the Constitutional Court.

February

After considering the reports of the sectoral regulator and the competition Tribunal, the government approves the merger of Endesa and Iberdrola under strongly restraining conditions. The merger is subsequently called off by the shareholders.

March

The government approves a labour market reform. Main measures include the liberalisation of part-time contracts, the extension of the permanent contract with lower severance payments introduced in 1997 to new groups of workers, and new severance payments for temporary contracts.

April

The government approves the re-balancing of Telefónica's tariffs, raising fixed and local variable prices and lowering international calls.

Following an agreement of one of the main trade unions (*Comisiones Obreras*) with the employers' association, the government approves a reform of the pension system to extend the 1996 Toledo Pact, which expires in 2001. The main measures include the extension of the possibility to retire early, the rise in minimum pensions for those under 65, the increase in survivors' replacement rate, and extended possibilities to work after age 65 (see Box 5).

Privatisation of the remaining stake of Iberia still in public hands (54 per cent).

The update of the Stability Program (2000-2004) maintains the objective of a surplus of 0.3 per cent of GDP for 2003, and extends it to 2004.

May

The social partners open negotiations to reform the collective wage bargaining system.

The government vetoes voting rights of two companies in *Hidrocantábrico*, the fourth largest electricity generator, after the success of their takeover bid on the company, arguing that they are publicly-owned foreign companies.

BASIC STATISTICS:

INTERNATIONAL COMPARISONS

	Units	Reference period[1]	Australia	Austria
Population				
Total	Thousands	1998	18 730	8 078
Inhabitants per sq. km	Number	1998	2	96
Net average annual increase over previous 10 years.............	%	1998	1.3	0.6
Employment				
Total civilian employment (TCE)[2]............................	Thousands	1998	8 596	3 689
of which:				
Agriculture..	% of TCE	1998	4.8	6.6
Industry	% of TCE	1998	21.9	31.8
Services	% of TCE	1998	73.3	61.7
Gross domestic product (GDP)				
At current prices and current exchange rates	Bill. US$	1998	372.7	210.9
Per capita	US$	1998	19 899	26 108
At current prices using current PPPs[3]	Bill. US$	1998	440.0	193.1
Per capita	US$	1998	23 492	23 900
Average annual volume growth over previous 5 years.............	%	1998	4.4	2.2
Gross fixed capital formation (GFCF)	% of GDP	1998	23.8	23.5
of which:				
Machinery and equipment	% of GDP	1998	10.3 (96)	9.3
Residential construction	% of GDP	1998	4.4 (96)	6.4
Average annual volume growth over previous 5 years.............	%	1998	2.7	0.2
Gross saving ratio[4]	% of GDP	1998	20.1	22.6
General government				
Current expenditure on goods and services	% of GDP	1998	18.2	19.8
Current disbursements[5]......................................	% of GDP	1998	32.0	47.8
Current receipts[6]	% of GDP	1998	33.3	47.7
Net official development assistance	% of GNP	1998	0.27	0.22
Indicators of living standards				
Private consumption per capita using current PPPs[3]	US$	1998	14 379	13 417
Passengers cars, per 1 000 inhabitants.........................	Number	1998	630	481
Internet hosts, per 1 000 inhabitants[7].........................	Number	1999	55	28
Television sets, per 1 000 inhabitants	Number	1998	495 (95)	331
Doctors, per 1 000 inhabitants................................	Number	1998	2.6	2.0
Infant mortality per 1 000 live births...........................	Number	1998	5.8 (96)	6.6
Wages and prices (average annual increase rate over previous 5 years)..				
Wages (earnings or rates according to availability)	%	1998	1.9	3.3
Consumer prices	%	1998	2.0	1.8
Foreign trade[8]				
Exports of goods, fob	Mill. US$	1998	55 885	62 742
As % of GDP..	%	1998	12.7	32.5
Average annual increase rate over previous 5 years	%	1998	5.7	9.3
Imports of goods, cif..	Mill. US$	1998	60 821	68 183
As % of GDP..	%	1998	13.8	35.3
Average annual increase rate over previous 5 years	%	1998	7.5	7.0
Total official reserves[9]	Mill. SDR's	1998	10 942	22 324
As ratio of average monthly imports of goods...................	Ratio	1998	2.2	4.3

1. Unless otherwise stated.
2. According to the definitions used in OECD *Labour Force Statistics.*
3. PPPs = Purchasing Power Parities.
4. Gross Saving = Gross national disposable income minus private and government consumption.

EMPLOYMENT OPPORTUNITIES

Economics Department, OECD

The Economics Department of the OECD offers challenging and rewarding opportunities to economists interested in applied policy analysis in an international environment. The Department's concerns extend across the entire field of economic policy analysis, both macroeconomic and microeconomic. Its main task is to provide, for discussion by committees of senior officials from Member countries, documents and papers dealing with current policy concerns. Within this programme of work, three major responsibilities are:

- to prepare regular surveys of the economies of individual Member countries;
- to issue full twice-yearly reviews of the economic situation and prospects of the OECD countries in the context of world economic trends;
- to analyse specific policy issues in a medium-term context for the OECD as a whole, and to a lesser extent for the non-OECD countries.

The documents prepared for these purposes, together with much of the Department's other economic work, appear in published form in the *OECD Economic Outlook, OECD Economic Surveys, OECD Economic Studies* and the Department's *Working Papers* series.

The Department maintains a world econometric model, INTERLINK, which plays an important role in the preparation of the policy analyses and twice-yearly projections. The availability of extensive cross-country data bases and good computer resources facilitates comparative empirical analysis, much of which is incorporated into the model.

The Department is made up of about 80 professional economists from a variety of backgrounds and Member countries. Most projects are carried out by small teams and last from four to eighteen months. Within the Department, ideas and points of view are widely discussed; there is a lively professional interchange, and all professional staff have the opportunity to contribute actively to the programme of work.

Skills the Economics Department is looking for:

a) Solid competence in using the tools of both microeconomic and macroeconomic theory to answer policy questions. Experience indicates that this normally requires the equivalent of a Ph.D. in economics or substantial relevant professional experience to compensate for a lower degree.

b) Solid knowledge of economic statistics and quantitative methods; this includes how to identify data, estimate structural relationships, apply basic techniques of time series analysis, and test hypotheses. It is essential to be able to interpret results sensibly in an economic policy context.

c) A keen interest in and extensive knowledge of policy issues, economic developments and their political/social contexts.

d) Interest and experience in analysing questions posed by policy-makers and presenting the results to them effectively and judiciously. Thus, work experience in government agencies or policy research institutions is an advantage.

e) The ability to write clearly, effectively, and to the point. The OECD is a bilingual organisation with French and English as the official languages. Candidates must have excellent knowledge of one of these languages, and some knowledge of the other. Knowledge of other languages might also be an advantage for certain posts.

f) For some posts, expertise in a particular area may be important, but a successful candidate is expected to be able to work on a broader range of topics relevant to the work of the Department. Thus, except in rare cases, the Department does not recruit narrow specialists.

g) The Department works on a tight time schedule with strict deadlines. Moreover, much of the work in the Department is carried out in small groups. Thus, the ability to work with other economists from a variety of cultural and professional backgrounds, to supervise junior staff, and to produce work on time is important.

General information

The salary for recruits depends on educational and professional background. Positions carry a basic salary from FF 318 660 or FF 393 192 for Administrators (economists) and from FF 456 924 for Principal Administrators (senior economists). This may be supplemented by expatriation and/or family allowances, depending on nationality, residence and family situation. Initial appointments are for a fixed term of two to three years.

Vacancies are open to candidates from OECD Member countries. The Organisation seeks to maintain an appropriate balance between female and male staff and among nationals from Member countries.

For further information on employment opportunities in the Economics Department, contact:

Management Support Unit
Economics Department
OECD
2, rue André-Pascal
75775 PARIS CEDEX 16
FRANCE

E-Mail: eco.contact@oecd.org

Applications citing ''ECSUR'', together with a detailed *curriculum vitae* in English or French, should be sent to the Head of Personnel at the above address.

For more information about all OECD publications
contact your nearest OECD Centre, or visit
www.oecd.org/bookshop

Pour plus d'informations sur les publications de l'OCDE,
contactez votre Centre OCDE le plus proche
ou visitez notre librairie en ligne :
www.oecd.org/bookshop

Where to send your request:
Où passer commande :

In Central and Latin America / En Amérique centrale et en Amérique du Sud

OECD MEXICO CENTRE / CENTRE OCDE DE MEXICO
Edificio INFOTEC
Av. San Fernando No. 37 Col. Toriello Guerra
Tlalpan C.P. 14050, Mexico D.F.
Tel.: +525 281 38 10   Fax: + 525 606 13 07
E-mail: mexico.contact@oecd.org   Internet: www.rtn.net.mx/ocde

In North America / En Amérique du Nord

OECD WASHINGTON CENTER / CENTRE OCDE DE WASHINGTON
2001 L Street N.W., Suite 650
Washington, DC 20036-4922
Tel.: +1 202 785-6323
Toll free / Numéro vert : +1 800 456-6323   Fax: +1 202 785-0350
E-mail: washington.contact@oecd.org   Internet: www.oecdwash.org

In Japan / Au Japon

OECD TOKYO CENTRE / CENTRE OCDE DE TOKYO
Landic Akasaka Bldg.
2-3-4 Akasaka, Minato-ku
Tokyo 107-0052
Tel.: +81 3 3586 2016   Fax: +81 3 3584 7929
E-mail : center@oecdtokyo.org   Internet: www.oecdtokyo.org

In the rest of the world / Dans le reste du monde

DVGmbH
Birkenmaarsstrasse 8
D-53340 Meckenheim
Germany
Tel.: +49 22 25 9 26 166/7/8   Fax: +49 22 25 9 26 169
E-mail: oecd@dvg.dsb.net

OECD Information Centre and Bookshop/
Centre d'information de l'OCDE et Librairie
OECD PARIS CENTRE / CENTRE OCDE DE PARIS
2 rue André-Pascal, 75775 Paris Cedex 16, France
Enquiries / Renseignements : Tel: +33 (0) 1 45 24 81 67
E-mail: sales@oecd.org

ONLINE BOOKSHOP / LIBRAIRIE EN LIGNE : **www.oecd.org/bookshop**

(secure payment with credit card / paiement sécurisé par carte de crédit)

OECD PUBLICATIONS, 2, rue André-Pascal, 75775 PARIS CEDEX 16
PRINTED IN FRANCE
(10 2001 03 1 P) ISBN 92-64-19137-2 – No. 51969 2001
ISSN 0376-6438